PRIMARY MATHEMATICS 2A
WORKBOOK

Marshall Cavendish
Education

SM SingaporeMath.com Inc®

Original edition published under the titles
Primary Mathematics Workbook 2A (Part One) and 2A (Part Two)
© 1981 Curriculum Planning & Development Division
Ministry of Education, Singapore
Published by Times Media Private Limited
This American Edition
© 2003 Times Media Private Limited
© 2003 Marshall Cavendish International (Singapore) Private Limited

Published by Marshall Cavendish Education
An imprint of Marshall Cavendish International (Singapore) Private Limited
Times Centre, 1 New Industrial Road, Singapore 536196
Customer Service Hotline: (65) 6411 0820
E-mail: tmesales@sg.marshallcavendish.com
Website: www.marshallcavendish.com/education

SM SingaporeMath.com Inc®
Distributed by
SingaporeMath.com Inc
404 Beavercreek Road #225
Oregon City, OR 97045
U.S.A.
Website: www.singaporemath.com

First published 2003
Second impression 2003
Third impression 2004
Reprinted 2004
Fourth impression 2005
Reprinted 2005 (twice), 2006 (twice), 2007 (twice), 2008, 2009 (twice),
          2010 (twice), 2011 (twice)

ISBN 978-981-01-8500-8

Printed in Singapore by Times Printers, www.timesprinters.com

ACKNOWLEDGEMENTS

Our special thanks to Richard Askey, Professor of Mathematics (University of Wisconsin, Madison), Yoram Sagher, Professor of Mathematics (University of Illinois, Chicago), and Madge Goldman, President (Gabriella and Paul Rosenbaum Foundation), for their indispensable advice and suggestions in the production of Primary Mathematics (U.S. Edition).

CONTENTS

1 Numbers to 1000

Exercise 1	7
Exercise 2	10
Exercise 3	12
Exercise 4	15
Exercise 5	19
Exercise 6	21
Exercise 7	24

2 Addition and Subtraction

Exercise 8	25
Exercise 9	26
Exercise 10	28
Exercise 11	30
Exercise 12	32
Exercise 13	35
Exercise 14	37
Exercise 15	40
Exercise 16	42
Exercise 17	44
Exercise 18	46
Exercise 19	49
Exercise 20	51

Exercise 21   54

Exercise 22   56

Exercise 23   59

Exercise 24   61

REVIEW 1   **63**

3 Length

Exercise 25   67

Exercise 26   68

Exercise 27   72

Exercise 28   74

REVIEW 2   **75**

4 Weight

Exercise 29   79

Exercise 30   81

REVIEW 3   **83**

REVIEW 4   **87**

5 Multiplication and Division

Exercise 31   91

Exercise 32   93

Exercise 33   95

Exercise 34   97

Exercise 35   99
Exercise 36   101
Exercise 37   103
Exercise 38   105
Exercise 39   107

REVIEW 5   **110**

6   Multiplication Tables of 2 and 3

Exercise 40   114
Exercise 41   118
Exercise 42   120
Exercise 43   122
Exercise 44   123
Exercise 45   125
Exercise 46   127
Exercise 47   129
Exercise 48   132
Exercise 49   134
Exercise 50   136

Exercise 51   138
Exercise 52   140
Exercise 53   142
Exercise 54   143
Exercise 55   145
Exercise 56   148
Exercise 57   150
Exercise 58   152
Exercise 59   154

Exercise 60   156
Exercise 61   158
Exercise 62   160

REVIEW 6   **163**

REVIEW 7   **169**

EXERCISE 1

1. Fill in the blanks.

(a)

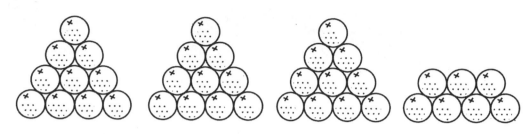

30 and 7 make __37__.

7 more than 30 is __37__.

30 + 7 = __37__

(b)

50 and 8 make __58__.

8 more than 50 is __58__.

50 + 8 = __5__

(c) 90 and 4 make _____.

4 more than 90 is _____.

90 + 4 = _____

2. Complete the number sentences.

(a) 40 + 9 =

(b) 60 + 2 =

(c) 70 + 10 =

(d) 90 + 10 =

3. Fill in the blanks.

(a)

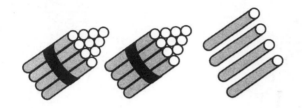

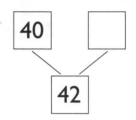

24 = _____ tens _____ ones

(b)

40 [ ]

42

42 = _____ tens _____ ones

(c)

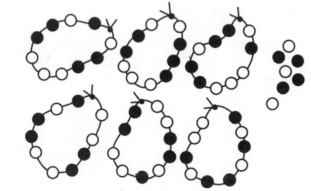

60 7

[ ]

67 = _____ tens _____ ones

4. Write the numbers.

(a) 4 tens 9 ones = _____

(b) 5 tens 2 ones = _____

(c) 6 tens 6 ones = _____

(d) 10 tens = _____

5. Write the numbers.

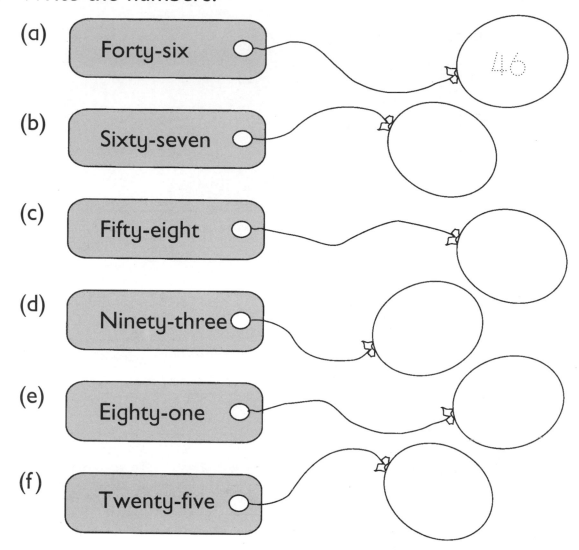

(a) Forty-six — 46

(b) Sixty-seven

(c) Fifty-eight

(d) Ninety-three

(e) Eighty-one

(f) Twenty-five

6. Write the numbers in words.

(a) 50 _____

(b) 64 _____

(c) 21 _____

(d) 99 _____

(e) 32 _____

(f) 100 _____

EXERCISE 2

Fill in the blanks.

1.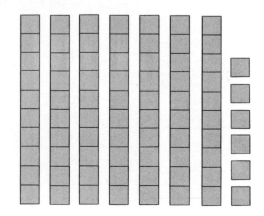

    (a) 1 more than 76 is _____ .

    (b) 1 less than 76 is _____ .

    (c) 10 more than 76 is _____ .

    (d) 10 less than 76 is _____ .

2. (a) 2 more than 76 is _____ .

    (b) 2 less than 76 is _____ .

    (c) 20 more than 76 is _____ .

    (d) 20 less than 76 is _____ .

3. (a) 2 more than 38 is _____ .

    (b) 10 more than 63 is _____ .

    (c) 20 more than 80 is _____ .

    (d) 2 less than 75 is _____ .

    (e) 10 less than 86 is _____ .

    (f) 20 less than 94 is _____ .

Complete the number sentences.

4.

(a) 55 + 1 =

(b) 55 + 2 =

(c) 55 + 10 =

(d) 55 + 20 =

(e) 55 − 1 =

(f) 55 − 2 =

(g) 55 − 10 =

(h) 55 − 20 =

5.

(a) 70 + 1 =

(b) 70 + 2 =

(c) 70 + 10 =

(d) 70 + 20 =

(e) 70 − 1 =

(f) 70 − 2 =

(g) 70 − 10 =

(h) 70 − 20 =

6.

(a) 48 + 1 =

(b) 48 + 2 =

(c) 48 + 10 =

(d) 48 + 20 =

(e) 48 − 1 =

(f) 48 − 2 =

(g) 48 − 10 =

(h) 48 − 20 =

EXERCISE 3

1. Circle the greater number.

(a)

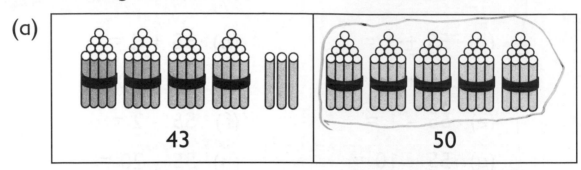

43   50

(b)

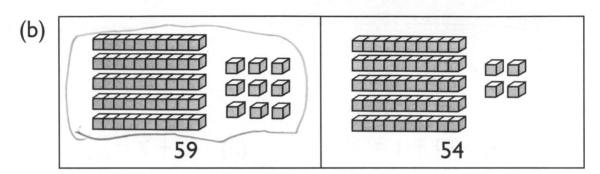

59   54

(c) | 28 | 26 | (d) | 70 | 65 |

(e) | 78 | 87 | (f) | 99 | 100 |

2. Circle the greatest number.

(a) | 43 | 45 | 42 | (b) | 78 | 87 | 85 |

(c) | 63 | 60 | 62 | (d) | 98 | 99 | 100 |

(e) | 59 | 70 | 62 | (f) | 57 | 52 | 54 |

3. Circle the smaller number.

(a)

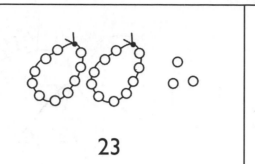

| 23 | 25 |

(b)

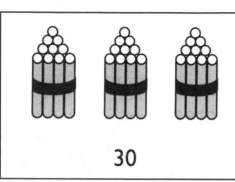

| 30 | 24 |

(c) | 31 | 29 | (d) | 78 | 87 |

(e) | 54 | 57 | (f) | 89 | 87 |

(g) | 63 | 60 | (h) | 98 | 100 |

4. Circle the smallest number.

(a) | 35 | 31 | 32 | (b) | 54 | 50 | 59 |

(c) | 45 | 50 | 47 | (d) | 59 | 56 | 66 |

(e) | 15 | 23 | 26 | (f) | 38 | 40 | 36 |

5. (a) Arrange the numbers in order.
Begin with the smallest.

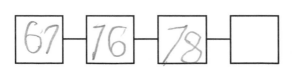 

67 — 76 — 78 — ☐

(b) Arrange the numbers in order.
Begin with the greatest.

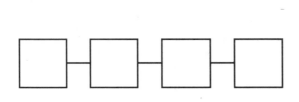 

☐ — ☐ — ☐ — ☐

6. Write **greater than (>)** or **less than (<)** in the blank.

(a) 44 is _____ 40.

(b) 50 is _____ 65.

(c) 62 is _____ 61.

(d) 70 is _____ 77.

(e) 39 is _____ 49.

(f) 58 is _____ 57.

(g) 73 is _____ 69.

(h) 65 is _____ 66.

(i) 24 is _____ 30.

(j) 47 is _____ 39.

EXERCISE 4

1. Write the numbers.

(a)

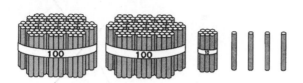

2 hundreds 1 ten 4 ones = _____

(b)

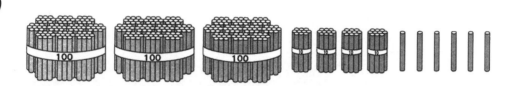

3 hundreds 4 tens 6 ones = _____

(c)

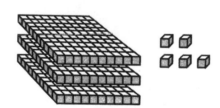

3 hundreds 5 ones = _____

(d) 4 hundreds 7 tens 2 ones = _____

(e) 5 hundreds 6 tens 3 ones = _____

(f) 6 hundreds 6 tens = _____

(g) 7 hundreds 9 tens = _____

(h) 3 hundreds 7 ones = _____

2. Match.

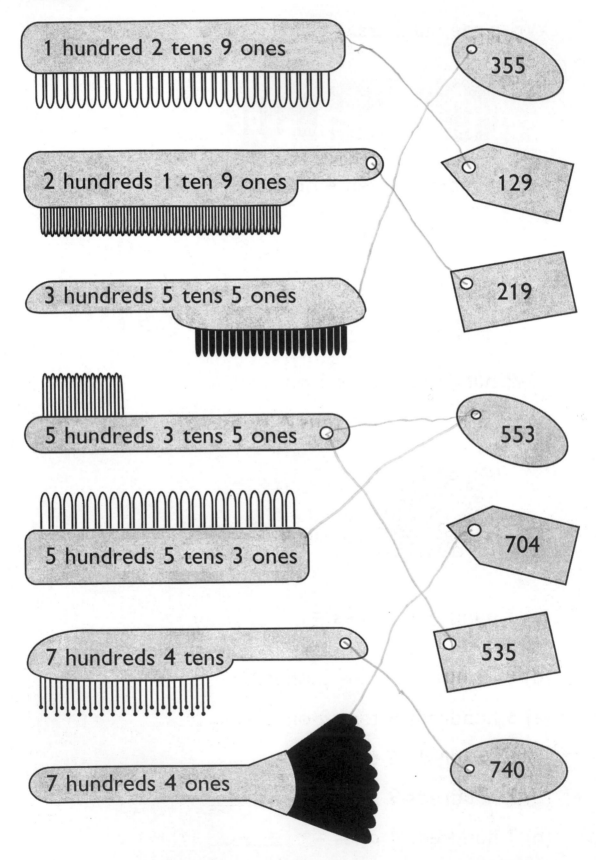

1 hundred 2 tens 9 ones

2 hundreds 1 ten 9 ones

3 hundreds 5 tens 5 ones

5 hundreds 3 tens 5 ones

5 hundreds 5 tens 3 ones

7 hundreds 4 tens

7 hundreds 4 ones

355

129

219

553

704

535

740

16

3. Write the numbers.

(a)

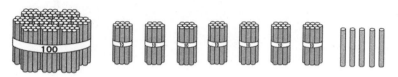

$100 + 70 + 5 = \underline{175}$

(b)

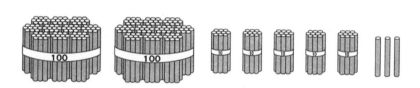

$200 + 50 + 3 = \underline{253}$

(c)

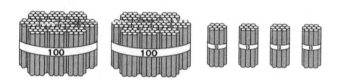

$200 + 40 = \underline{240}$

(d)

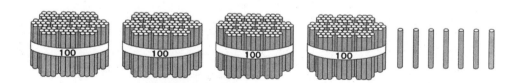

$400 + 7 = \underline{407}$

4. Write the missing numbers.

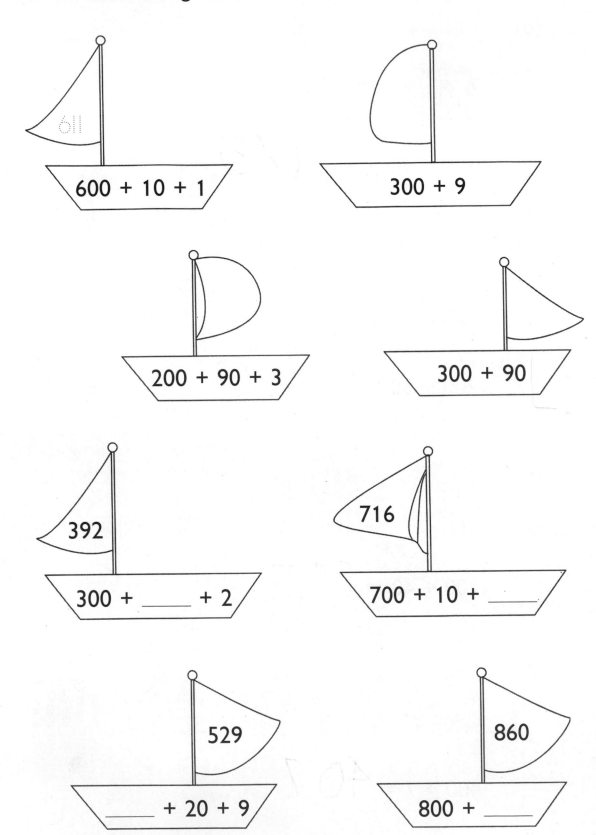

600 + 10 + 1

300 + 9

200 + 90 + 3

300 + 90

392
300 + _____ + 2

716
700 + 10 + _____

529
_____ + 20 + 9

860
800 + _____

18

EXERCISE 5

1. Write the amount of money.

    (a)

    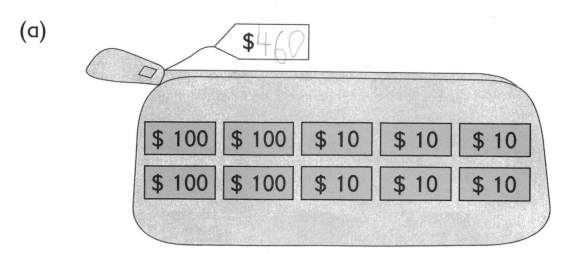

    $460

    (b)

    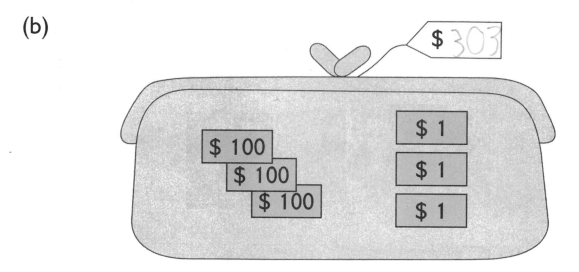

    $303

    (c)

    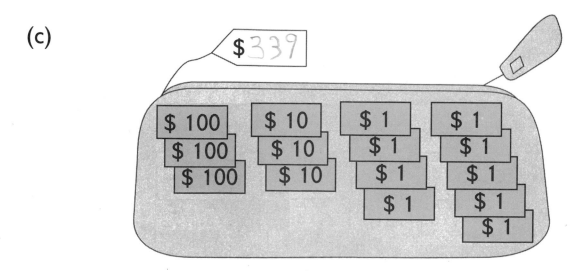

    $339

2. What number does each chart show?

(a)

Hundreds	Tens	Ones
	10 10 10 10 10	1 1 1 1 1 1

_____

(b)

Hundreds	Tens	Ones
100 100 100	10 10	1 1 1 1 1

_____

(c)

Hundreds	Tens	Ones
100 100 100 100 100 100 100	10 10 10 10 10 10	1

_____

(d)

Hundreds	Tens	Ones
100 100 100 100	10 10 10	

_____

(e)

Hundreds	Tens	Ones
100 100 100 100 100 100		1 1 1 1 1 1

_____

EXERCISE 6

1. Match.

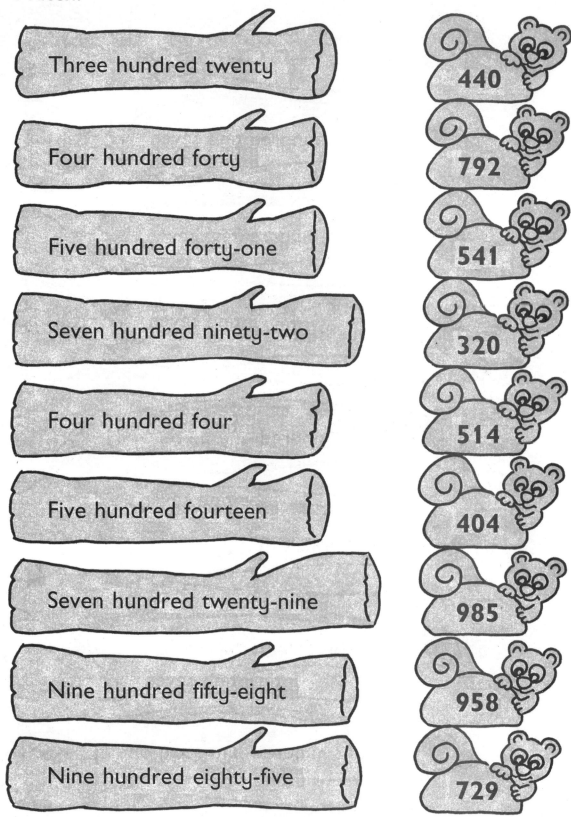

Three hundred twenty — 440

Four hundred forty — 792

Five hundred forty-one — 541

Seven hundred ninety-two — 320

Four hundred four — 514

Five hundred fourteen — 404

Seven hundred twenty-nine — 985

Nine hundred fifty-eight — 958

Nine hundred eighty-five — 729

2. Write the numbers.

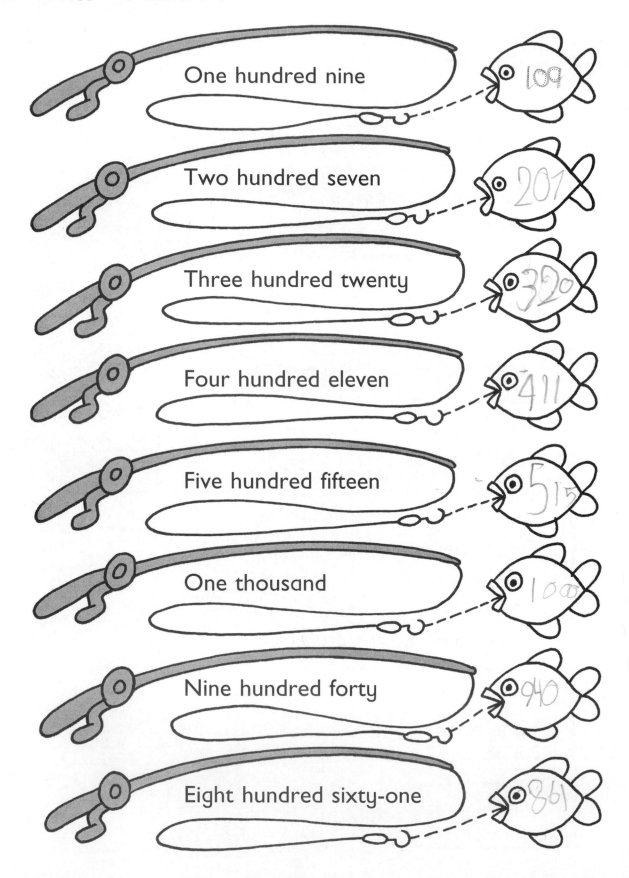

One hundred nine — 109

Two hundred seven — 207

Three hundred twenty — 320

Four hundred eleven — 411

Five hundred fifteen — 515

One thousand — 1000

Nine hundred forty — 940

Eight hundred sixty-one — 861

3. Fill in the blanks with the correct words.

Three hundred thirteen
Five hundred sixty
Seven hundred ninety-nine
Four hundred forty-one
Six hundred fifty-five
Eight hundred four

804 _____

441 _____

313 _____

799 _____

655 _____

560 _____

4. Write the numbers in words.

680 _____

821 _____

909 _____

253 _____

312 _____

EXERCISE 7

Fill in the blanks.

1. (a)

Hundreds	Tens	Ones
100 100 100	10 10	1 1 1 1 1

10

10 more than 325 is __335__ .

(b)

Hundreds	Tens	Ones
100 100 100 100	10 10	

10

10 less than 430 is __420__ .

(c)

Hundreds	Tens	Ones
100 100 100 100 100		1 1 1 1 1 1

100

100 less than 606 is __506__ .

2. (a) What number is 10 more than 563? __573__

(b) What number is 10 less than 784? __774__

(c) What number is 100 more than 408? __508__

(d) What number is 100 less than 940? __840__

EXERCISE 8

1. Add or subtract.

(a) 8 + 2 = 10
    2 + 8 = 10
    10 − 2 = 8
    10 − 8 = 2

(b) 4 + 7 = 11
    7 + 4 = 11
    11 − 4 = 7
    11 − 7 = 4

(c) 7 + 6 = 13
    6 + 7 = 13
    13 − 6 = 19
    13 − 7 = 20

(d) 6 + 8 = 14
    8 + 6 = 14
    14 − 8 = 22
    14 − 6 = 8

(e) 14 + 3 = 17
    3 + 14 = 17
    17 − 3 = 14
    17 − 14 = 3

(f) 10 + 9 = 19
    9 + 10 = 19
    19 − 10 = 9
    19 − 9 = 10

(g) 20 + 5 = 25
    5 + 20 = 25
    25 − 5 = 20
    25 − 20 = 5

(h) 13 + 6 = 19
    6 + 13 = 19
    19 − 6 = 13
    19 − 13 = 6

EXERCISE 9

1. Compare the two sets.

    (a)

    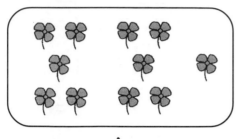
    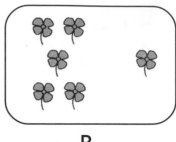

A	B

    11 − 6 = _5_

    Set A has _5_ flowers more than Set B.

    (b)

    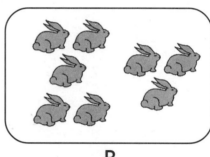

A	B

    15 − 8 = _7_

    Set B has _7_ rabbits less than Set A.

    (c)

    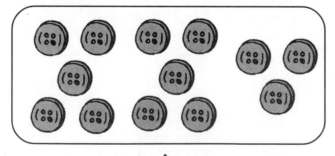
    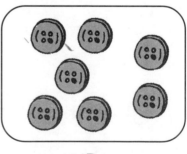

A	B

    13 − 7 = _6_

    Set B has _6_ buttons less than Set A.

2. Fill in the blanks.

(a) $12 - 4 = $ _8_

4 less than 12 is _8_ .

(b) $16 - 9 = $ _6_

9 less than 16 is _6_ .

(c) $17 - 8 = $ _9_ .

_9_ is 8 less than 17.

(d) $14 - 6 = $ _8_

_8_ is 6 less than 14.

(e) $11 - 7 = $ _4_

_4_ is 7 less than 11.

(f) $13 - 5 = $ _8_

_8_ is 5 less than 13.

EXERCISE 10

1. Mrs. Chen made 45 buns.
   She sold 31 of them.
   How many buns did she have left?

   $$45 - 31 = 14$$

   She had ___14___ buns left.

---

2. Jill bought 24 green apples and 37 red apples.
   How many more red apples than green apples did
   she buy?

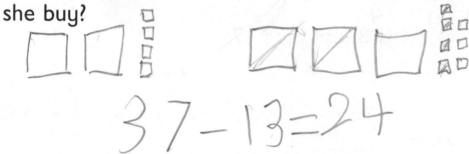

   $$37 - 13 = 24$$

   She bought ___13___ more red apples than green
   apples.

---

3. Ryan is 23 years old.
   He is 24 years younger than his father.
   How old is his father?

   $$23 + 24 = 47$$

   His father is ___47___ years old.

4.

(a) Samy bought the book and pen.
He spent $ 34 .

(b) The train set cost $ 12 more than
the doll.

(c) David had $86.
He bought the watch.
He had $ 71 left.

(d) Sumin had $30.
He wanted to buy the book.
He needed $ 2 more.

29

EXERCISE 11

1. Fill in the blanks.

(a)

5 ones

3 ones

5 ones + 3 ones = ___8___ ones

5 + 3 = ___8___

(b)

5 tens

3 tens

5 tens + 3 tens = ___80___ tens

50 + 30 = ___80___

(c)

5 hundreds

3 hundreds

5 hundreds + 3 hundreds = ___8___ hundreds

500 + 300 = ___800___

2. Add.

(a)   3 + 4   = 7

    30 + 40   = 70

    300 + 400 = 700

(b)   8 + 2   = 10

    80 + 20   = 100

    800 + 200 = 1000

3. Add and write the answers in the boxes.

ACROSS

A. 50 + 6   5 6
B. 38 + 11   4 9
D. 27 + 30   5 7
F. 26 + 63   8 9
H. 73 + 2   7 5
J. 55 + 13
K. 24 + 24
M. 14 + 63
N. 25 + 51
O.   4 + 91
P. 23 + 41

DOWN

A. 53 + 5
C. 96 + 2
E. 21 + 34
G. 91 + 8
H. 41 + 31
I. 13 + 25
J. 61 + 6
K. 14 + 32
L. 37 + 32
N. 31 + 43

31

8/31

EXERCISE 12

1. Add.

501 + 97 *598* **A**	384 + 12 *396* **C**	730 + 57 *787* **E**
165 + 24 *189* **H**	810 + 46 *856* **M**	422 + 73 *495* **N**
601 + 54 *655* **O**	746 + 43 *789* **R**	941 + 30 *971* **T**

*84
+12
96*

What did one wall say to the other wall?

Write the letters in the boxes below to find out.

M	e	e	t
856	787	787	971

m	e
856	787

A	t
598	971

t	H	e
971	189	787

C	o	r	N	e	r
396	655	789	495	787	789

2. Add.

648 + 201 849	436 + 231 667	700 + 135 835
540 + 249 789	625 + 173 798	213 + 153 366
107 + 381 488	445 + 124 569	657 + 330 987

Where is Maggie going?

Color the spaces which contain the answers to find out.

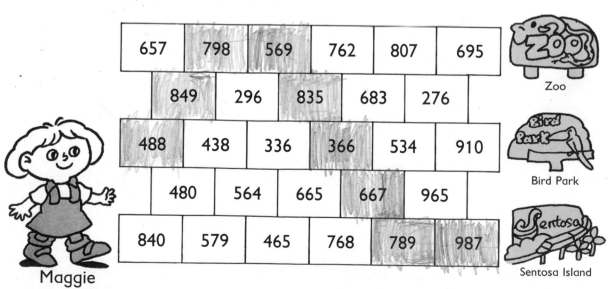

Maggie

Zoo

Bird Park

Sentosa Island

33

3. David has 410 U.S. stamps.
   He has 56 Canadian stamps.
   How many stamps does he have altogether?

   410 + 56 =

   He has _____ stamps altogether.

4. Lily has 125 stickers.
   Her brother has 63 stickers more than she.
   How many stickers does her brother have?

   Her brother has _____ stickers.

5. After selling 242 books, Mr. Cohen had 304 books left.
   How many books did he have at first?

   He had _____ books at first.

EXERCISE 13

1. Fill in the blanks.

(a)

8 ones – 2 ones = _____ ones

8 – 2 = _____

(b)

8 tens – 2 tens = _____ tens

80 – 20 = _____

(c)

8 hundreds – 2 hundreds = _____ hundreds

800 – 200 = _____

2. Subtract.

(a) 7 – 3   =

70 – 30   =

700 – 300 =

(b) 10 – 1   =

100 – 10 =

1000 – 100 =

3. Subtract and write the answers in the boxes.

	A 7	B 5		C	D
E		F 3	G		
H	I		J	K	
				L	M
N		O			
P				Q	

ACROSS

A. 96 − 21

C. 65 − 41

F. 38 − 6

H. 47 − 20

J. 26 − 12

L. 98 − 10

O. 73 − 23

P. 67 − 31

Q. 55 − 53

DOWN

B. 85 − 32

D. 57 − 14

E. 78 − 6

G. 34 − 13

I. 89 − 15

K. 99 − 51

M. 87 − 3

N. 95 − 42

EXERCISE 14

1. Subtract.

689 − 32	786 − 73	979 − 71
145 − 25	379 − 53	589 − 40
896 − 62	259 − 14	460 − 60

Color the spaces which contain the answers.
You will help the rabbit find its way home.

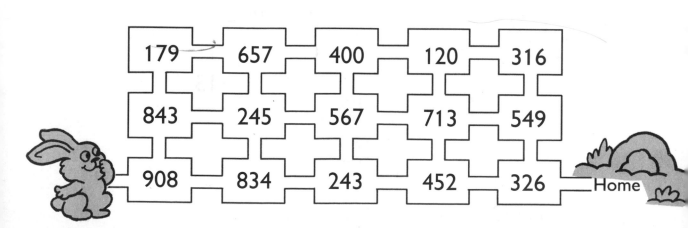

179	657	400	120	316
843	245	567	713	549
908	834	243	452	326

Home

2. Subtract.

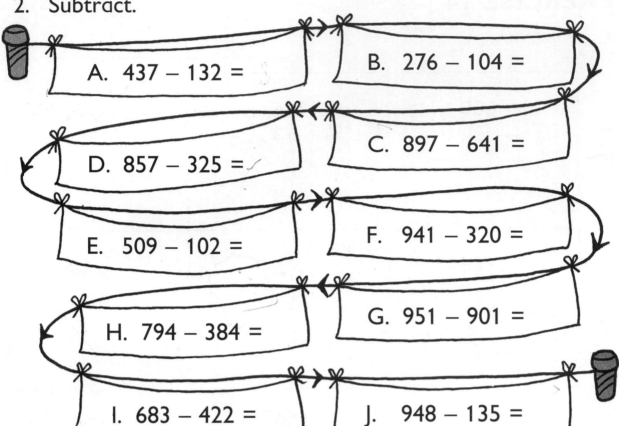

A. 437 − 132 =

B. 276 − 104 =

C. 897 − 641 =

D. 857 − 325 =

E. 509 − 102 =

F. 941 − 320 =

G. 951 − 901 =

H. 794 − 384 =

I. 683 − 422 =

J. 948 − 135 =

Join the dots by following the order of the answers above.

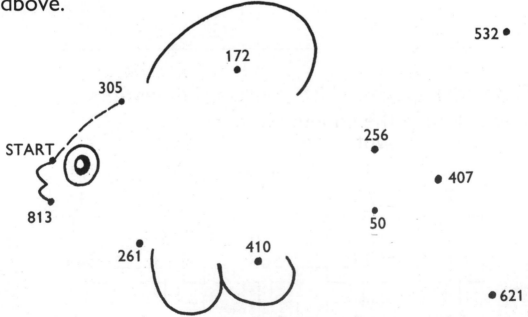

532

172

305

256

407

START

813

50

261

410

621

You will get a picture of a _____ .

3. A tailor bought 68 buttons.
    He used 43 of them.
    How many buttons did he have left?

    He had _____ buttons left.

___

4. Morgan saved $276.
    She saved $54 more than Lily.
    How much money did Lily save?

    Lily saved $ _____ .

___

5. Courtney went shopping with $563.
    She bought a watch and had $142 left.
    How much did she pay for the watch?

    She paid $ _____ for the watch.

EXERCISE 15

1. Add.

(a) 7 + 6 = 27 + 6 = 527 + 6 =	(b) 3 + 7 = 43 + 7 = 243 + 7 =
(c) 5 + 8 = 50 + 80 = 450 + 80 =	(d) 9 + 1 = 90 + 10 = 390 + 10 =
(e) 8 + 9 = 68 + 9 = 268 + 9 =	(f) 6 + 4 = 86 + 4 = 386 + 4 =

2. Add.

(a) 65 + 6 =   (b) 79 + 2 =

(c) 138 + 7 =   (d) 637 + 3 =

(e) 90 + 60 =   (f) 30 + 70 =

(g) 230 + 80 =   (h) 460 + 40 =

3. Add.

$$62 + 19$$ A

$$67 + 25$$ B

$$45 + 48$$ D

$$25 + 47$$ H

$$43 + 39$$ I

$$79 + 16$$ P

$$46 + 38$$ R

$$36 + 34$$ T

$$51 + 29$$ Y

Write the letters which match the answers.
You will find a message.

	A			
72	81	95	95	80

						A	
92	82	84	70	72	93	81	80

EXERCISE 16

1. Add.

913 + 68	234 + 139	402 + 69
527 + 266	703 + 169	328 + 48
605 + 145	346 + 329	836 + 54

Color the spaces which contain the answers.
You will help Mr. Lion find the way to the river.

2. Add.

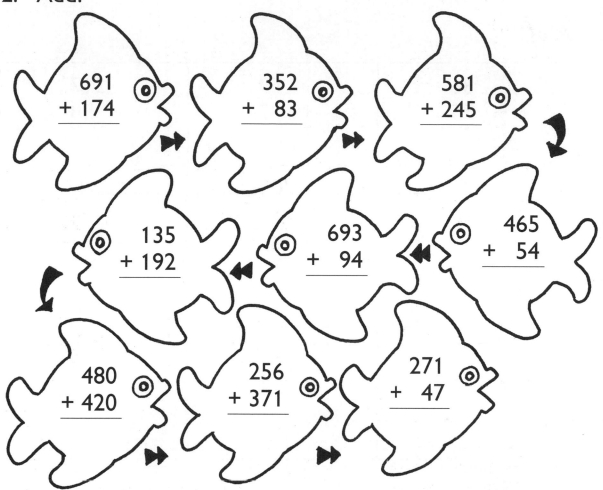

Join the dots by following the order of the answers above.
You will get a picture of an _____.

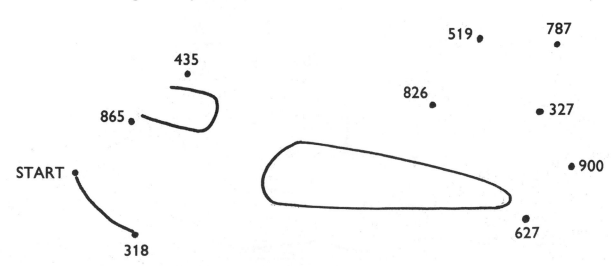

EXERCISE 17

1. Add.

36 + 55	49 + 7	317 + 38
128 + 3	461 + 62	206 + 274
543 + 281	152 + 251	607 + 245

Which animal is Alice's pet?
Color the spaces that contain the answers to find out.

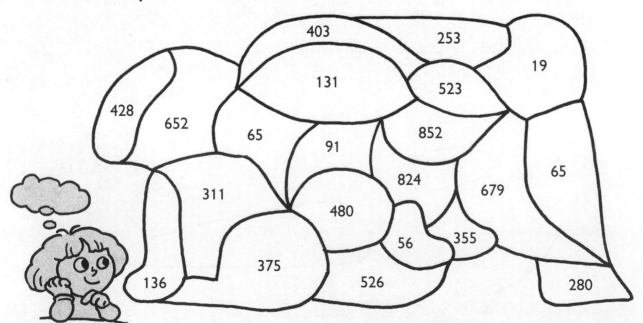

2. Sumin has 231 picture cards.
   His friend gives him 19 more.
   How many picture cards does he have now?

   He has _____ picture cards now.

3. There are 285 men and 72 women in a club.
   How many people are there in the club?

   There are _____ people in the club.

4. Lily saved $162.
   Weilin saved $360.
   How much money did they save altogether?

   They saved $ _____ altogether.

EXERCISE 18

1. Add.

763 + 57 **C**	286 + 39 **D**	802 + 99 **E**	426 + 75 **G**
178 + 195 **H**	361 + 279 **L**	367 + 535 **T**	595 + 265 **Z**

Match each letter with an animal to check the answers.

640

820

325

860

501

902

373

901

46

2. Add.

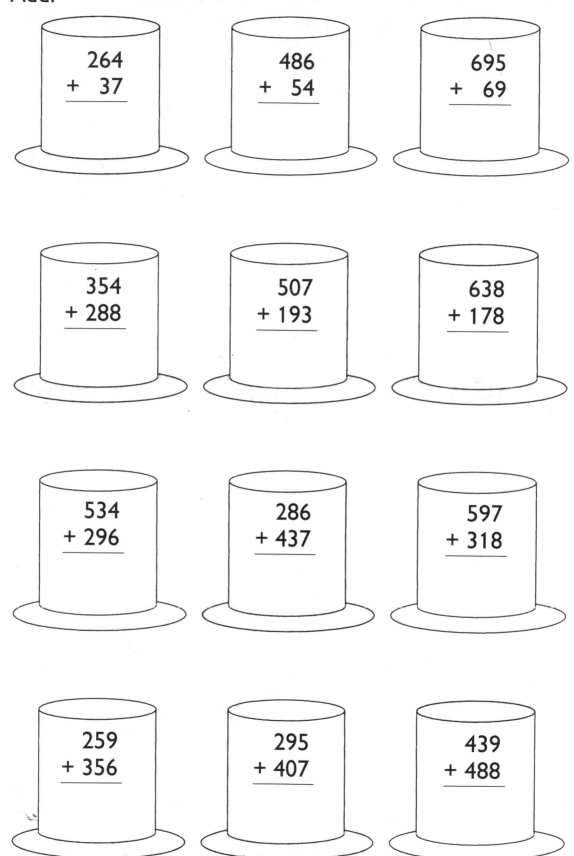

264	486	695
+ 37	+ 54	+ 69
354	507	638
+ 288	+ 193	+ 178
534	286	597
+ 296	+ 437	+ 318
259	295	439
+ 356	+ 407	+ 488

3. After spending $82, Matthew had $139 left.
   How much money did he have at first?

   He had $ _____ at first.

---

4. Mrs. Bates bought an oven for $393.
   She also bought a refrigerator for $438.
   How much did she spend altogether?

   She spent $ _____ altogether.

---

5. There are 468 desks in a hall.
   There are 156 more chairs than desks.
   How many chairs are there in the hall?

   There are _____ chairs in the hall.

EXERCISE 19

1. Add.

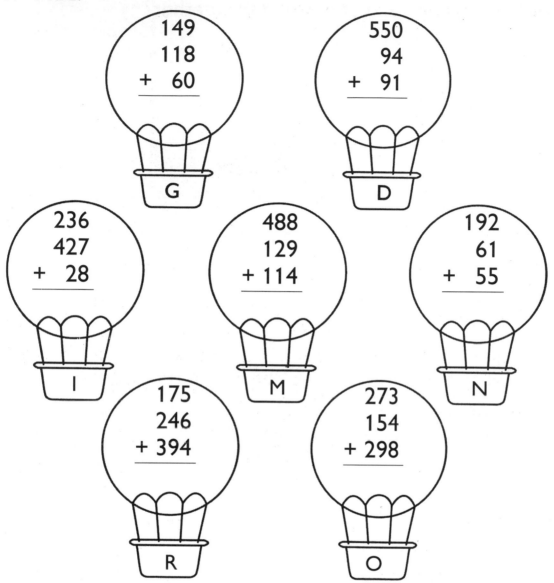

$$\begin{array}{r} 149 \\ 118 \\ + \ \ 60 \\ \hline \end{array}$$
G

$$\begin{array}{r} 550 \\ 94 \\ + \ \ 91 \\ \hline \end{array}$$
D

$$\begin{array}{r} 236 \\ 427 \\ + \ \ 28 \\ \hline \end{array}$$
I

$$\begin{array}{r} 488 \\ 129 \\ + 114 \\ \hline \end{array}$$
M

$$\begin{array}{r} 192 \\ 61 \\ + \ \ 55 \\ \hline \end{array}$$
N

$$\begin{array}{r} 175 \\ 246 \\ + 394 \\ \hline \end{array}$$
R

$$\begin{array}{r} 273 \\ 154 \\ + 298 \\ \hline \end{array}$$
O

Write the letters in the boxes below.
You will find a message.

G			
327	725	725	735

						G
731	725	815	308	691	308	327

2. Mrs. Kennedy made 95 apple tarts, 98 pineapple tarts and 57 orange tarts.
   How many tarts did she make altogether?

   She made _____ tarts altogether.

3. This chart shows the number of books in a library.

English books	408
Science books	274
History books	224

   What is the total number of books in the library?

   The total number of books is _____ .

4. A watch costs $167.
   A camera costs $48 more than the watch.
   What is the cost of the camera?

   The cost of the camera is $ _____ .

EXERCISE 20

1. Subtract.

52 − 37 **C**	74 − 36 **D**	83 − 46 **E**
96 − 57 **I**	62 − 58 **M**	45 − 39 **N**
50 − 4 **O**	87 − 59 **S**	90 − 64 **T**

Why do you go to bed?
Write the letters in the boxes below to find the reason.

☐ ☐   ☐ ☐ ☐ ☐   ☐ ☐ ☐
39 26   38 46 37 28   6   46 26

☐ ☐ ☐ ☐   ☐ ☐   ☐ ☐
15 46 4 37   26 46   4 37

51

2. Subtract.

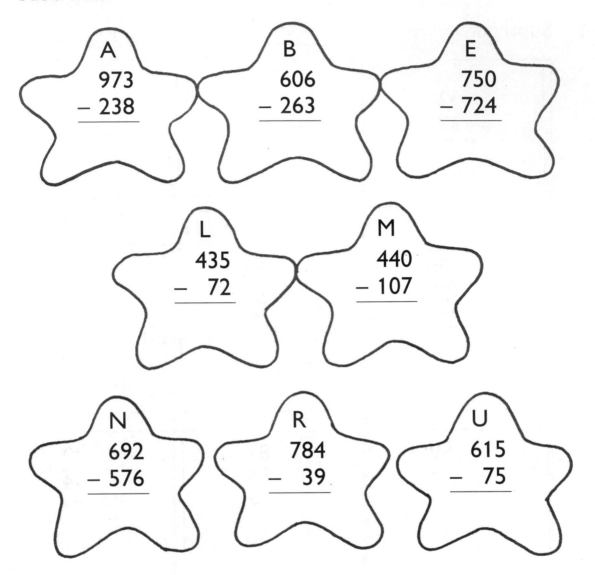

A
973
− 238

B
606
− 263

E
750
− 724

L
435
− 72

M
440
− 107

N
692
− 576

R
784
− 39

U
615
− 75

What goes up when the rain comes down?
Write the letters in the boxes below to find out.

A	
735	116

							A
540	333	343	745	26	363	363	735

52

3. Roger had $186.
   He spent $38 at a bookshop.
   How much money did he have left?

   He had $ _____ left.

---

4. There were 132 melons in a basket.
   34 of them were rotten.
   How many melons were **not** rotten?

   _____ melons were not rotten.

---

5. Sara collected 150 stamps.
   Nicole collected 43 fewer stamps than Sara.
   How many stamps did Nicole collect?

   Nicole collected _____ stamps.

EXERCISE 21

1. Subtract.

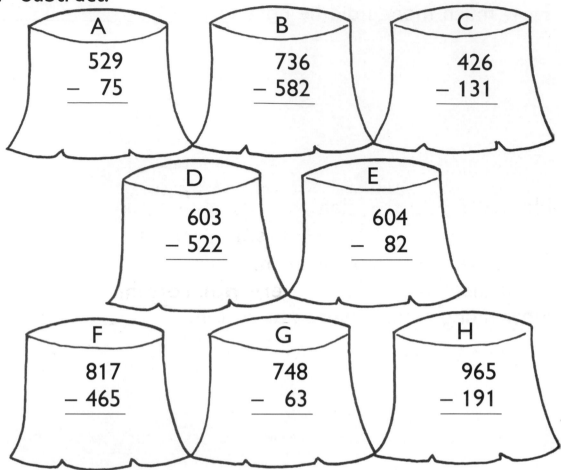

A	B	C
529	736	426
− 75	− 582	− 131

D	E
603	604
− 522	− 82

F	G	H
817	748	965
− 465	− 63	− 191

Write the words which match the answers.
You will find a message.

A	B	C	D
___	___	___	___

E	F	G	H
___	___	___	___

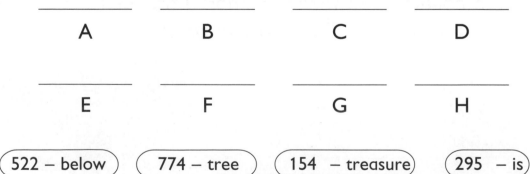

522 – below   774 – tree   154 – treasure   295 – is

454 – the   685 – rain   81 – hidden   352 – the

54

2. There are **968** students in a school.
    395 of them wear glasses.
    How many students do **not** wear glasses?

    _____ students do not wear glasses.

3. Meiling has $474.
    Her sister has $282 less than she.
    How much money does her sister have?

    Her sister has $ _____ .

4. Ali made 345 sticks of chicken satay and 128 sticks of beef satay.
    How many more sticks of chicken satay than beef satay did Ali make?

    Ali made _____ more sticks of chicken satay than beef satay.

EXERCISE 22

1. Subtract.

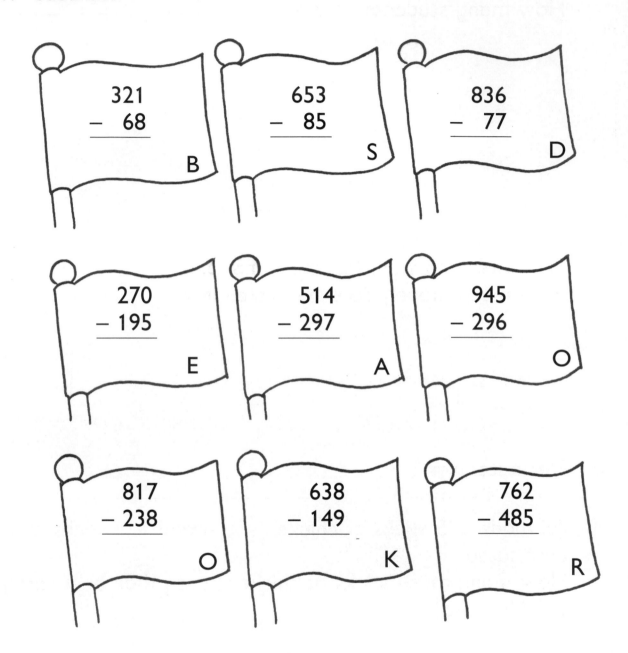

| | 321 |
| | − 68 |

B

| | 653 |
| | − 85 |

S

| | 836 |
| | − 77 |

D

| | 270 |
| | − 195 |

E

| | 514 |
| | − 297 |

A

| | 945 |
| | − 296 |

O

| | 817 |
| | − 238 |

O

| | 638 |
| | − 149 |

K

| | 762 |
| | − 485 |

R

Write the letters in the boxes below to complete the message.

277	75	217	759		253	579	649	489	568

2. Subtract.

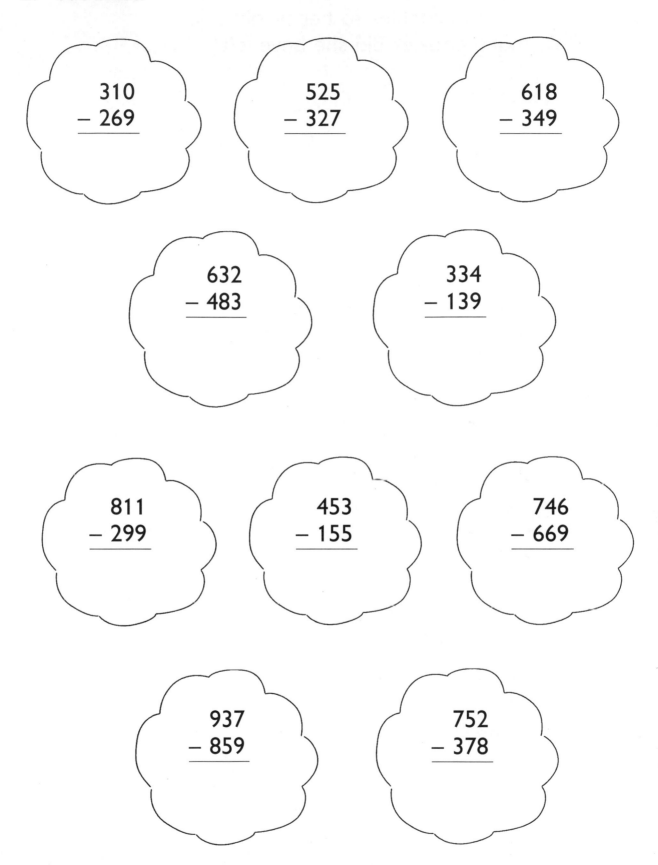

$$310 - 269$$

$$525 - 327$$

$$618 - 349$$

$$632 - 483$$

$$334 - 139$$

$$811 - 299$$

$$453 - 155$$

$$746 - 669$$

$$937 - 859$$

$$752 - 378$$

3. Ashley made 415 cookies.
   She gave 158 cookies to her neighbors.
   How many cookies did she have left?

   She had _____ cookies left.

4. There are 250 houses in Orchid Estate.
   There are 174 houses in Rose Estate.
   How many more houses are there in Orchid Estate
   than in Rose Estate?

   There are _____ more houses in Orchid Estate than
   in Rose Estate.

5. Mrs. Garcia went shopping with $620.
   She spent $565.
   How much money did she have left?

   She had $ _____ left.

EXERCISE 23

1. Subtract.
    Then write the letters which match the answers.
    You will find out where the water is.

306 − 38 268	300 − 162
I	

700 − 338	803 − 257	105 − 79

901 − 242	800 − 774	500 − 15	604 − 119

26	546	268	485	138	362	659
E	H	I	L	N	T	W

2. Mrs. Smith made 700 cookies and muffins.
   There were 369 cookies.
   How many muffins were there?

   There were _____ muffins.

3. Mr. Chen had 504 pears.
   After selling some of them, he had 286 pears left.
   How many pears did he sell?

   He sold _____ pears.

4. There are 207 cars in Parking Lot A.
   There are 179 cars in Parking Lot B.
   How many more cars are there in Parking Lot A than
   in Parking Lot B?

   There are _____ more cars in Parking Lot A than in
   Parking Lot B.

EXERCISE 24

1. Add or subtract.

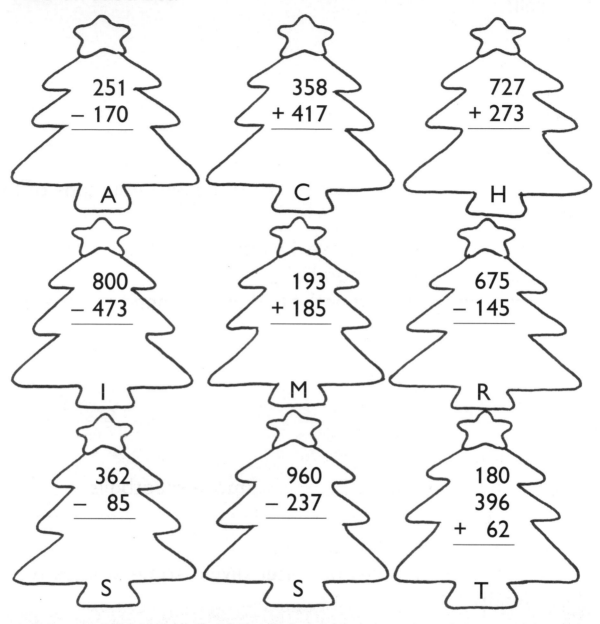

	251 − 170 = A	358 + 417 = C	727 + 273 = H
800 − 473 = I	193 + 185 = M	675 − 145 = R
362 − 85 = S	960 − 237 = S	180 396 + 62 = T

Write the letters in the boxes below to complete the message.

M E R R Y

							A	
775	1000	530	327	277	638	378	81	723

2. Eric sold 296 cups of coffee and 158 cups of tea.
   How many more cups of coffee than cups of tea did he sell?

   He sold _____ more cups of coffee than cups of tea.

3. Mrs. Lin wants to make 150 meatballs for a party.
   She has made 78 meatballs.
   How many more meatballs does she need to make?

   She needs to make _____ more meatballs.

4. David collected 930 stamps.
   He had 845 stamps left after giving some stamps to his friends.
   How many stamps did he give to his friends?

   He gave _____ stamps to his friends.

REVIEW 1

1. Match.

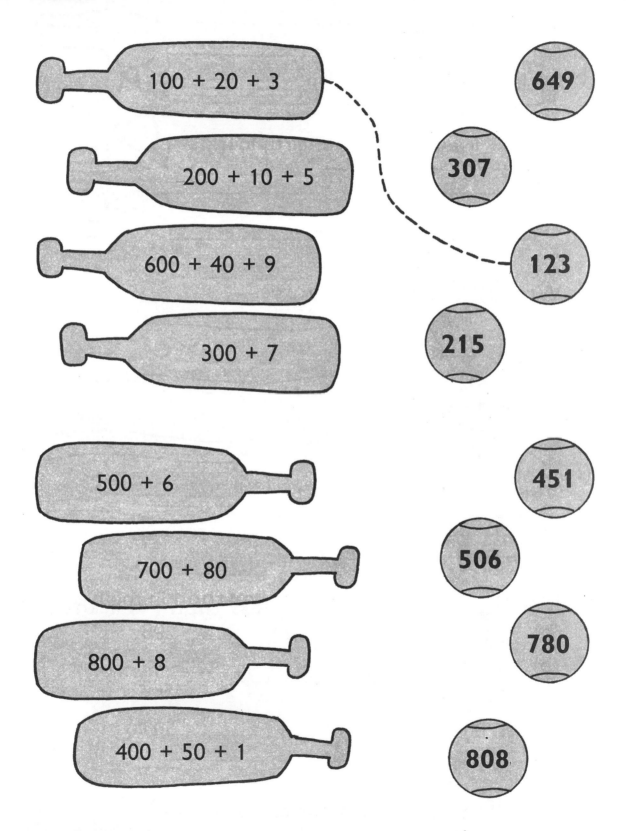

100 + 20 + 3

200 + 10 + 5

600 + 40 + 9

300 + 7

649

307

123

215

500 + 6

700 + 80

800 + 8

400 + 50 + 1

451

506

780

808

2. Write the numbers.

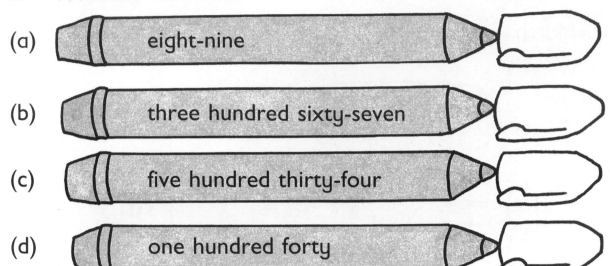

(a) eight-nine

(b) three hundred sixty-seven

(c) five hundred thirty-four

(d) one hundred forty

3. Write the numbers in words.

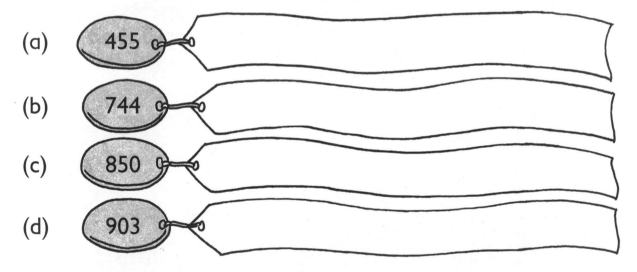

(a) 455

(b) 744

(c) 850

(d) 903

4. Write **greater than (>)** or **less than (<)** in the blank.

(a) 210 is _____ 208.

(b) 399 is _____ 402.

(c) 465 is _____ 456.

(d) 520 is _____ 502.

(e) 755 is _____ 750.

(f) 925 is _____ 900.

5. Write the missing numbers.

(a)

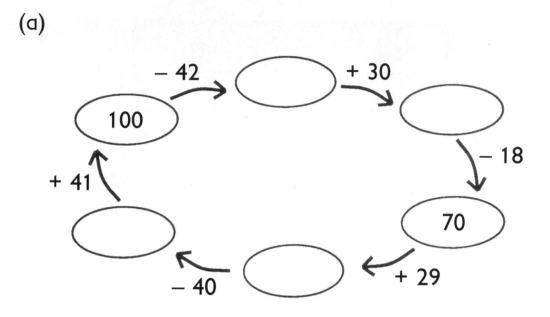

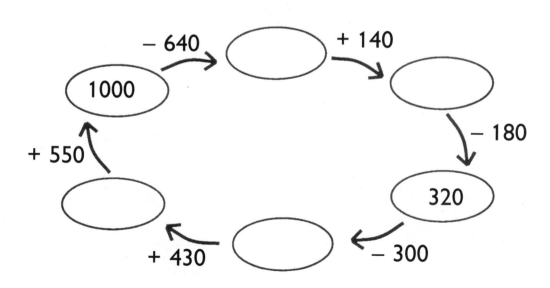

6. The chart shows the number of people in a club.

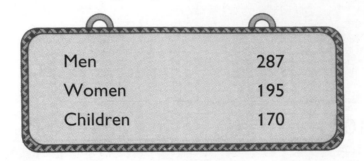

Men	287
Women	195
Children	170

(a) How many adults are there in the club?

There are _____ adults in the club.

(b) How many more men than women are there?

There are _____ more men than women.

(c) How many people are there altogether?

There are _____ people altogether.

EXERCISE 25

1. Work with your friends.
    Cut a string which you think is 1 m long.
    Then check the length of your string with a meter rule.

2. You need a meter rule or a string which is 1 m long.
    Put a (✓) in the correct box.

	Less than 1 m	More than 1 m
My height		
My reach		
Length of my desk		
Width of my desk		
Height of my desk		

3. You need a meter rule or a string which is 1 m long.
    Estimate and then measure the following lengths.

	My estimate	My measure
Length of the chalkboard	about _____ m	about _____ m
Length of one side of the classroom	about _____ m	about _____ m

EXERCISE 26

1. Estimate and then measure the following lengths.

	My estimate	My measure
Length of my textbook	about _____ cm	about _____ cm
Length of my pencil	about _____ cm	about _____ cm
Length of my pencil case	about _____ cm	about _____ cm
Length of a drinking straw	about _____ cm	about _____ cm

2. How many centimeters long are these things?

(a)

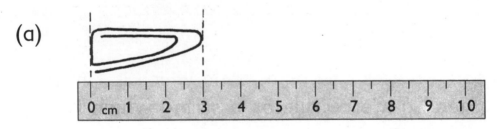

The paper clip is _____ cm long.

(b)

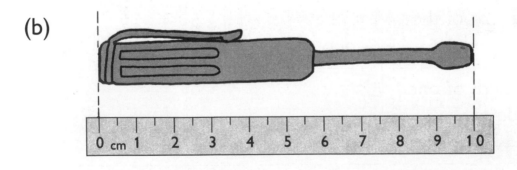

The screwdriver is _____ cm long.

3. Use your ruler to measure the length in centimeters.

(a)

The key is about _____ cm long.

(b)

The toothbrush is about _____ cm long.

(c)

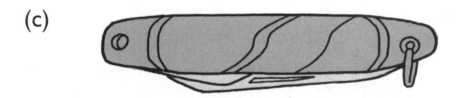

The penknife is about _____ cm long.

(d)

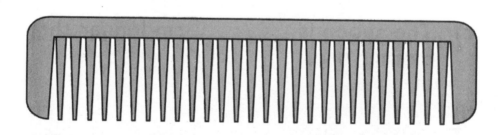

The comb is about _____ cm long.

4. Fill in the blanks.

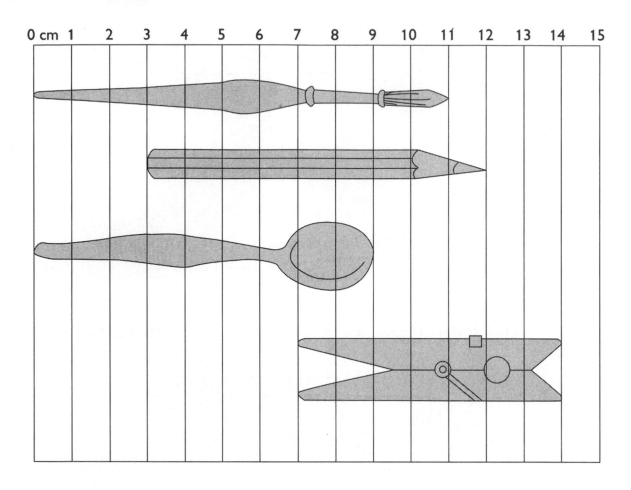

(a) The brush is _____ cm long.

(b) The pencil is _____ cm long.

(c) The spoon is _____ cm longer than the clothes pin.

(d) The clothes pin is _____ cm shorter than the brush.

(e) The _____ is the longest.

(f) The _____ is the shortest.

5. Fill in the blanks with cm or m.

(a) The height of a flagpole
   is 5 _____ .

(b) The height of a coconut tree
   is 10 _____ .

(c) The length of an exercise book is 21 _____ .

(d) The length of a pencil box is 23 _____ .

(e) The height of a girl is 1 _____ .

(f) The height of a bottle is 20 _____ .

(g) Mr. Wu is 165 _____ tall.

(h) Lily uses a piece of ribbon
   40 _____ long to make a bow.

(i) The length of a swimming pool is 50 _____ .

(j) Ali is 4 _____ taller than his brother.

EXERCISE 27

1. Work with your friends.
    Use a measuring tape to measure your waist.
    Then measure the waists of three friends.

    Complete the table.

Name	Length of waist
	about _____ cm
	about _____ cm
	about _____ cm
	about _____ cm

2. Measure the lines in centimeters.

    (a)

    Line A is about _____ cm long.

    (b)

    Line B is about _____ cm long.

    (c) Line A is about _____ cm longer than Line B.

3. Measure the length and width of this rectangle.

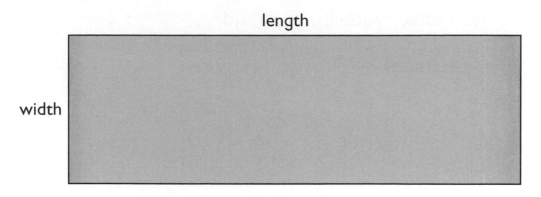

length

width

The length is about _____ cm.

The width is about _____ cm.

4. Use a string and a ruler to measure the lines.

(a)

A

Line A is about _____ cm long.

(b)

B

Line B is about _____ cm long.

(c)
C

Line C is about _____ cm long.

(d) Line _____ is the longest.

(e) Line _____ is the shortest.

EXERCISE 28

1. Fill in the blanks with in., ft or yd.

    (a) The length of a television is about 2 _____.

    (b) The length of a paper clip is about 1 _____.

    (c) The length of a classroom chalkboard is about

    3 _____.

    (d) A pencil is about 7 _____ long.

    (e) Emma is about 3 _____ tall.

2. A green rod is 2 yd long. A yellow rod is 2 m long.

    Which rod is longer? _____

3. _____
    A   B

    (a) Draw a line 3 in. longer than AB.

    (b) Draw a line 2 in. shorter than AB.

REVIEW 2

1. Write the missing numbers.

(a)

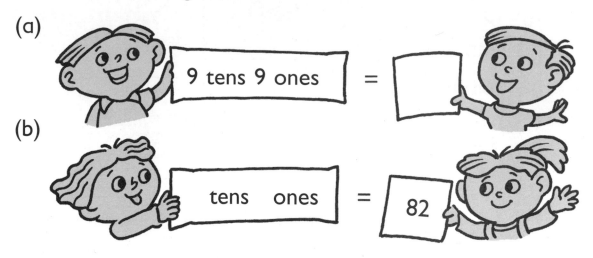

9 tens 9 ones ☐ = ☐

(b)

☐ tens ☐ ones = 82

(c) ☐ hundreds ☐ tens ☐ ones = 647

(d) ☐ hundreds ☐ tens ☐ ones = 503

2. Arrange these numbers in order.
   Begin with the smallest.

904   899
908   910

_____ _____ _____ _____

3. Write the missing numbers.

994		996	997		
	985				
			977		
				968	
	955	956			
	945			948	

4. Write **greater than (>)** or **less than (<)** in the blank.

   (a) 601 is _____ 599.

   (b) 689 is _____ 710.

   (c) 740 is _____ 700.

   (d) 560 is _____ 506.

   (e) 413 is _____ 453.

   (f) 388 is _____ 380.

5. Add.

   (a)

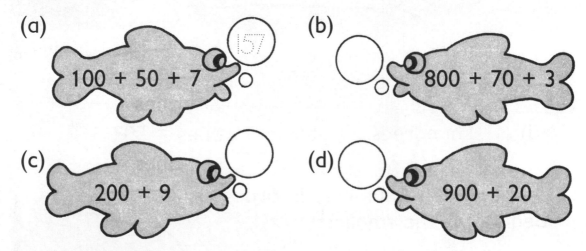

   100 + 50 + 7   157

   (b)   800 + 70 + 3

   (c)   200 + 9

   (d)   900 + 20

6. Write the amount of money.

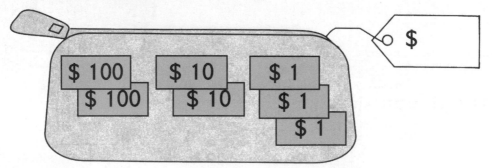

   $ 100 $ 10 $ 1
   $ 100 $ 10 $ 1
                    $ 1

   $

7. Write the missing numbers.

   (a) 600 + ☐ = 630   (b) 500 + ☐ = 542

   (c) 408 − ☐ = 400   (d) 750 − ☐ = 650

8. (a) What number is 1 more than 999? _____

    (b) What number is 10 more than 790? _____

    (c) What number is 10 less than 700? _____

    (d) What number is 100 more than 208? _____

    (e) What number is 100 less than 342? _____

9. Write the numbers.

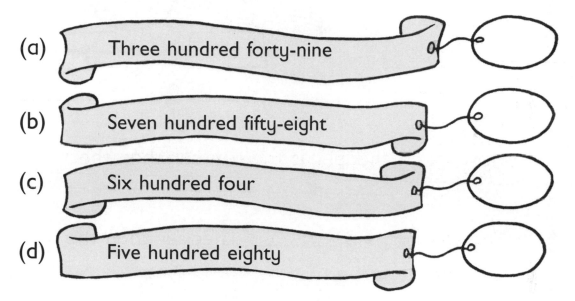

    (a) Three hundred forty-nine

    (b) Seven hundred fifty-eight

    (c) Six hundred four

    (d) Five hundred eighty

10. Write the numbers in words.

    (a) 220 _____

    (b) 431 _____

    (c) 869 _____

    (d) 944 _____

11.

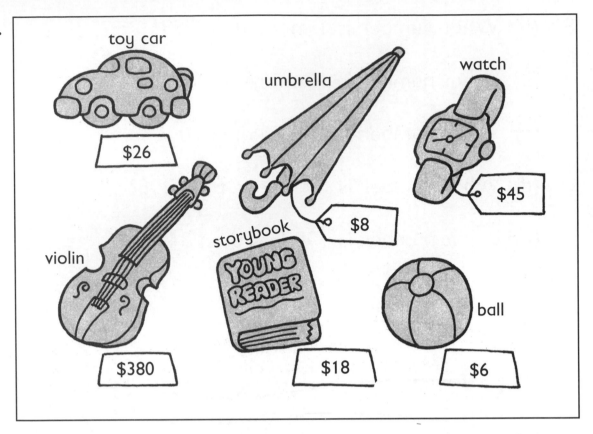

(a) How much cheaper is the toy car than the watch?

The toy car is $ _____ cheaper than the watch.

(b) Mary bought the violin and the storybook. How much did she spend altogether?

She spent $ _____ altogether.

(c) Lily bought the toy car, the ball and the umbrella. How much did she spend in all?

She spent $ _____ in all.

78

EXERCISE 29

1. Work with your friends.
   You need a weighing scale.
   Get an object which you
   think weighs about 1 kg.
   Then check the weight of
   the object with the weighing scale.

2. You need a weighing scale.
   Put a tick (✓) in the correct box.

	less than 1 kg	more than 1 kg
Weight of a pair of shoes		
Weight of 5 textbooks		

3. Fill in the blanks.

The _____ weighs more than 1 kg.

The _____ weigh 1 kg.

The _____ weigh less than 1 kg.

4. How much does each weigh?

(a)

_____ kg

(b)

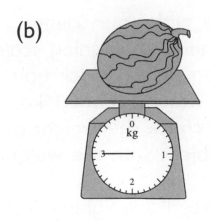

_____ kg

(c)

_____ kg

(d)

_____ kg

(e)

_____ kg

(f)

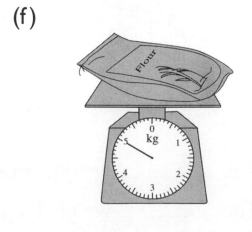

_____ kg

EXERCISE 30

1. Work with your friends.
    You need a weighing scale.
    Estimate the weight of each of the following.
    Then check by weighing.

	My estimate	My measure
a pencil	about _____ g	about _____ g
a mug	about _____ g	about _____ g
10 marbles	about _____ g	about _____ g

2. Fill in the blanks.

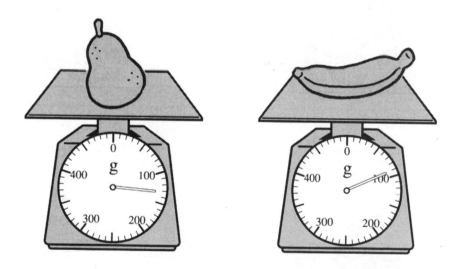

(a) The pear weighs _____ g.

(b) The banana weighs _____ g.

(c) The total weight of the fruits is _____ g.

(d) The pear weighs _____ g more than the banana.

3. How much does each weigh?

(a)

_____ g

(b)

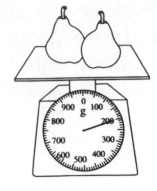

_____ g

(c)

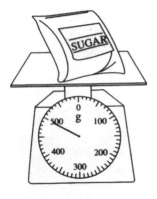

_____ g

(d)

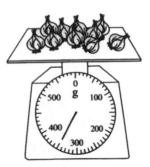

_____ g

(e)

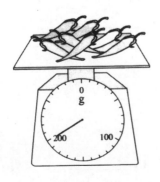

_____ g

(f)

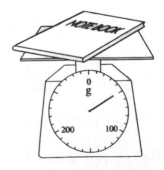

_____ g

REVIEW 3

1. Add or subtract.

   (a) 100 + 90 + 2 =   (b) 200 + 9 =

   (c) 300 + 70 =   (d) 400 + 5 =

   (e) 566 − 500 =   (f)   665 − 60 =

   (g) 798 − 400 =   (h)   999 − 90 =

2. Write the missing numbers.

   (a) 300 + ☐ + 8 = 398

   (b) 400 + 60 + ☐ = 467

   (c) ☐ + 2 = 702

   (d) ☐ + 40 = 240

3. Write two addition sentences and two subtraction sentences using the numbers in the bag.

   ☐ + ☐ = ☐

   ☐ + ☐ = ☐

   ☐ − ☐ = ☐

   ☐ − ☐ = ☐

100
62   38

4. Add or subtract.

(a) 263 + 126 =	(b) 805 − 305 =
(c) 330 + 86 =	(d) 450 − 48 =
(e) 469 + 531 =	(f) 622 − 567 =

5. Write the missing numbers.

(a) 228 $\xrightarrow{+ 300}$ ☐

(b) 309 $\xrightarrow{+ 60}$ ☐

(c) 451 $\xrightarrow{+ 500}$ ☐

(d) 569 $\xrightarrow{- 200}$ ☐

(e) 674 $\xrightarrow{- 40}$ ☐

6. After reading 285 pages of a book, Meihua still has 167 pages to read.
How many pages are there in the book?

There are _____ pages in the book.

7. John collected 635 postcards.
He collected 165 fewer postcards than David.
How many postcards did David collect?

David collected _____ postcards.

8. Siti made 600 apple tarts.
She made 485 pineapple tarts.
How many more apple tarts than pineapple tarts did she make?

She made _____ more apple tarts than pineapple tarts.

9. 148 men, 137 women and 359 children went to the zoo.
   How many people went to the zoo?

   _____ people went to the zoo.

---

10. Raja paid $305 for a camera and a calculator.
    The calculator cost $59.
    What was the cost of the camera?

    The cost of the camera was $ _____ .

---

11. Devi used 580 beads to make a handbag.
    She still had 85 beads left.
    How many beads did she have at first?

    She had _____ beads at first.

REVIEW 4

1. Color the spaces which contain the answer **1000** to make a picture.

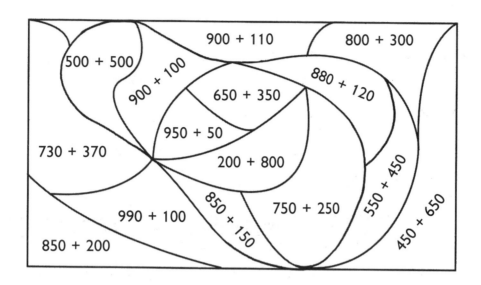

2. Write the greatest number and the smallest number using all the 3 digits.

	greatest number	smallest number
4, 0, 2	420	204
3, 4, 1		
5, 4, 7		
4, 2, 3		
5, 4, 9		
3, 0, 3		

3. Write the missing numbers.

(a) 600 + 80 + 9 = ☐

(b) 200 + ☐ + 8 = 248

(c) 389 − ☐ = 309

(d) 407 − ☐ = 207

4. How long is each?

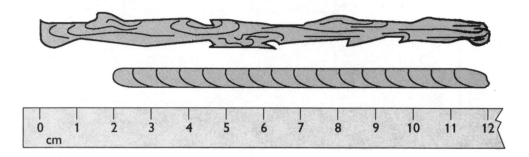

The stick is _____ cm long.

The rope is _____ cm long.

5. How heavy is each?

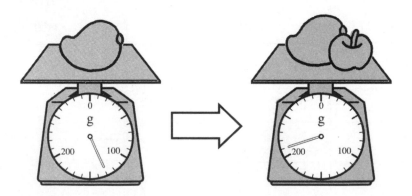

(a) The mango weighs _____ g.

(b) The apple weighs _____ g.

6. 312 boys and 295 girls took part in a swimming test. How many more boys than girls were there?

There were _____ more boys than girls.

7. There are 292 men, 149 women and 68 children on a train.
How many people are there on the train?

There are _____ people on the train.

8. Meihua and her sister saved $502 altogether.
Meihua saved $348.
How much did her sister save?

Her sister saved $ _____ .

9. A washing machine costs $650.
   Mrs. Bates has $527.
   How much more money does she need to buy the washing machine?

   She needs $ _____ more.

10. A papaya weighs 860 g.
    A mango is 280 g lighter than the papaya.
    What does the mango weigh?

    The mango weighs _____ g.

11. Find the total length of the 3 sides of the triangle.

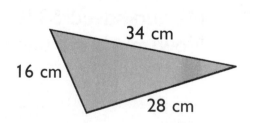

    The total length is _____ cm.

EXERCISE 31

1. Fill in the blanks.

    (a)

    3 eights = _____

    3 × 8 = _____

    (b)

    8 threes = _____

    8 × 3 = _____

    (c)

    5 fours = _____

    5 × 4 = _____

2. Fill in the blanks.

(a)

2 groups of 7 = _____

2 × 7 = _____

(b)

7 groups of 2 = _____

7 × 2 = _____

(c)

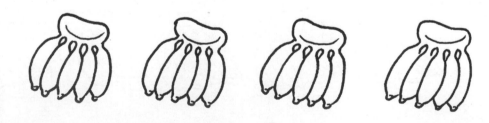

4 groups of 5 = _____

4 × 5 = _____

EXERCISE 32

1. Multiply 2 by 5.

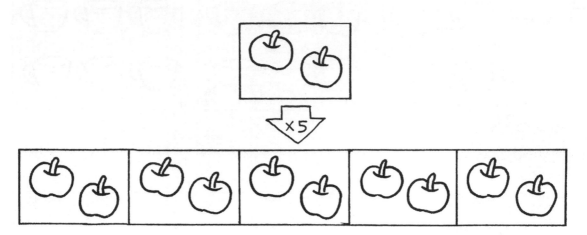

$$2 \times 5 =$$

2. Multiply 4 by 2.

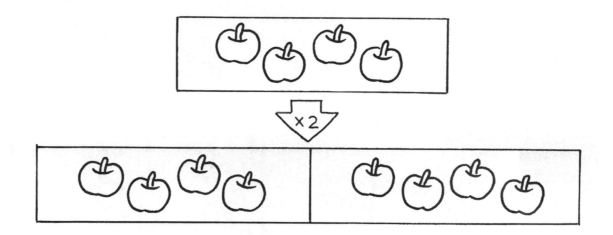

$$4 \times 2 =$$

3. Multiply 6 by 3.

$6 \times 3 =$

---

4. Multiply 8 by 3.

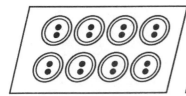 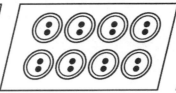 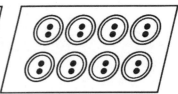

$8 \times 3 =$

---

5. Multiply 7 by 4.

$7 \times 4 =$

EXERCISE 33

1. There are 4 stars on each card.

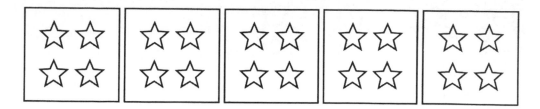

$4 \times 5 =$

There are _____ stars altogether.

2. There are 6 cakes in each box.

$6 \times 2 =$

There are _____ cakes altogether.

3. There are 8 flowers in each vase.

$8 \times 3 =$

There are _____ flowers altogether.

4. A fly has 6 legs.
   How many legs do 4 flies have?

   6 × 4 =

   4 flies have _____ legs.

---

5. There are 6 bottles in each row.
   How many bottles are there in 3 rows?

   6 × 3 =

   There are _____ bottles altogether.

---

6. There are 10 buttons on each card.
   How many buttons are there on 5 cards?

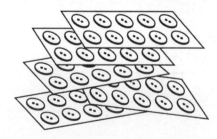

   10 × 5 =

   There are _____ buttons altogether.

EXERCISE 34

1. Complete the multiplication sentences.

(a)

5 × 3 =   3 × 5 =

(b)

7 × 2 =   2 × 7 =

(c)

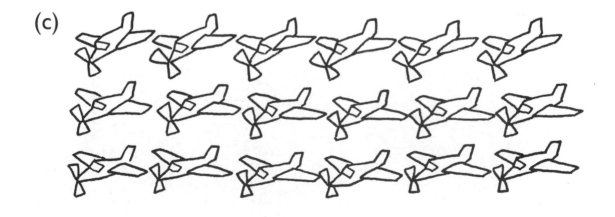

6 × 3 =   3 × 6 =

2. Complete the multiplication sentences.

(a)

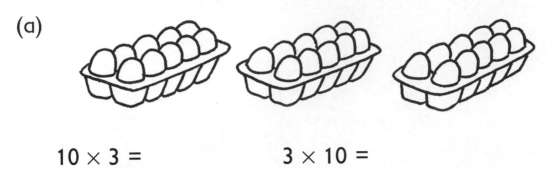

10 × 3 =   3 × 10 =

(b)

7 × 4 =   4 × 7 =

(c)

8 × 6 =   6 × 8 =

(d)

10 × 3 =   3 × 10 =

EXERCISE 35

1. Fill in the blanks.

   (a)

   Divide 12 apples into 2 equal groups.

   There are _____ apples in each group.

   (b)

   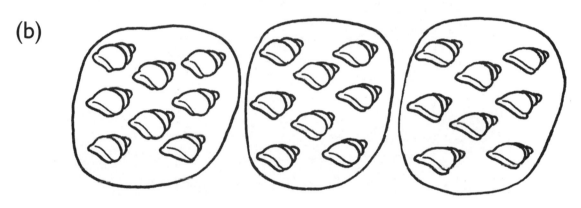

   Divide 24 shells into 3 equal groups.

   There are _____ shells in each group.

   (c)

   Divide 20 flowers into 5 equal groups.

   There are _____ flowers in each group.

2. (a)

Divide 10 rabbits into 2 equal groups.

There are _____ rabbits in each group.

(b) 10 ÷ 2 = _____

3. (a)

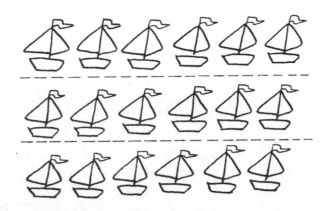

Divide 18 boats into 3 equal groups.

There are _____ boats in each group.

(b) 18 ÷ 3 = _____

4. Divide.

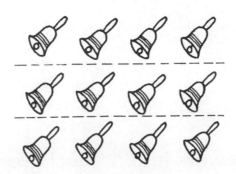

12 ÷ 3 = _____

EXERCISE 36

1. Divide.

(a)

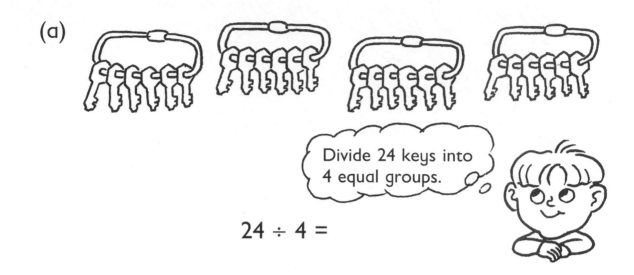

Divide 24 keys into 4 equal groups.

24 ÷ 4 =

(b)

21 ÷ 3 =

(c)

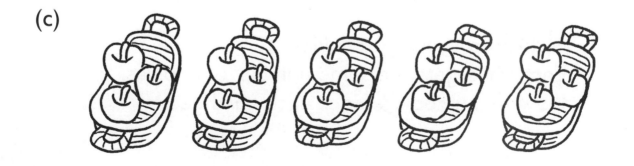

15 ÷ 5 =

2.

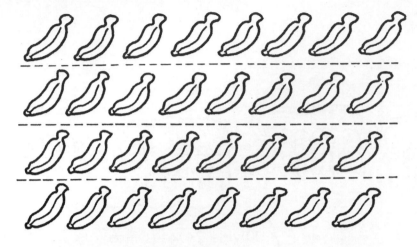

A monkey ate 32 bananas in 4 days.
It ate the same number of bananas each day.
How many bananas did it eat a day?

$$\boxed{} \div \boxed{} = \boxed{}$$

It ate _____ bananas a day.

3.

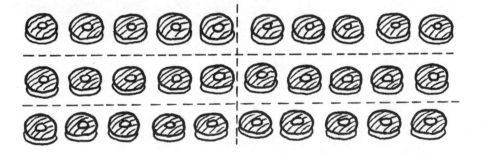

6 children share 30 cookies.
Each child gets the same number of cookies.
How many cookies does each child get?

$$\boxed{} \div \boxed{} = \boxed{}$$

Each child gets _____ cookies.

EXERCISE 37

1. Fill in the blanks.

    (a)

    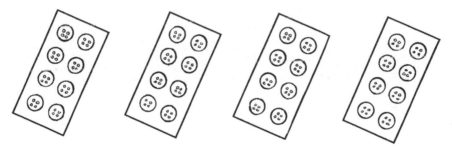

    Divide 30 stones into groups of 10.

    There are _____ groups.

    (b) Divide 32 buttons into groups of 8.

    There are _____ groups.

    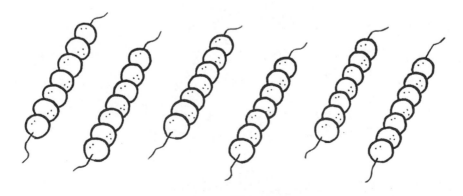

    (c) Divide 42 beads into groups of 7.

    There are _____ groups.

103

2. (a) Divide 15 apples into groups of 5.

There are _____ groups.

(b) 15 ÷ 5 = _____

3. (a) Divide 28 butterflies into groups of 4.

There are _____ groups.

(b) 28 ÷ 4 = _____

4. Divide.

18 ÷ 6 = _____

EXERCISE 38

1. Divide.

(a)

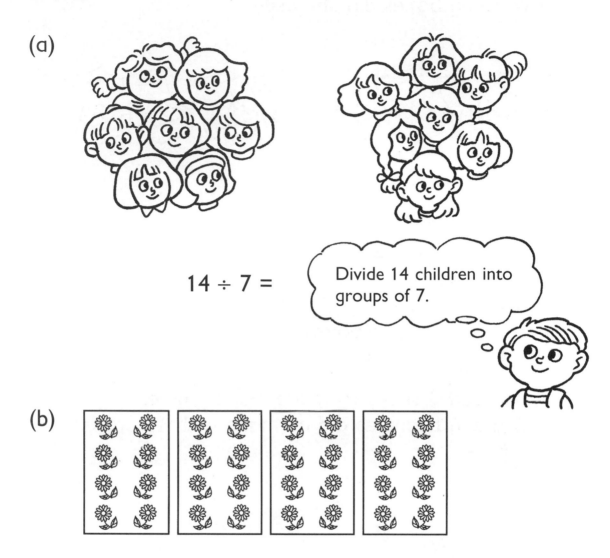

$14 \div 7 =$

Divide 14 children into groups of 7.

(b)

$32 \div 8 =$

(c)

$27 \div 9 =$

2. Jamie bought **18** pastries.
   She put **2** pastries in a box.
   How many boxes did she use?

$$\square \div \square = \square$$

She used _____ boxes.

---

3. David used **3** sticks to make one triangle.
   How many triangles did he make with **15** sticks?

$$\square \div \square = \square$$

He made _____ triangles.

EXERCISE 39

1. There are 30 buns.

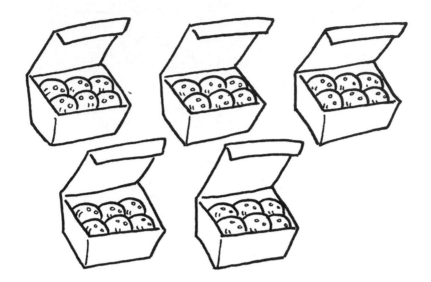

(a) Put the buns equally into 5 boxes.
    How many buns are there in each box?

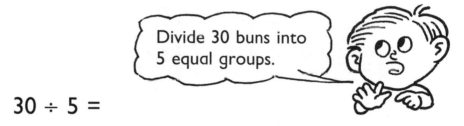

Divide 30 buns into 5 equal groups.

$30 \div 5 =$

There are _____ buns in each box.

(b) Put 6 buns in each box.
    How many boxes are there?

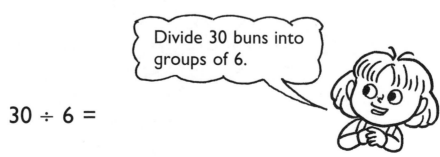

Divide 30 buns into groups of 6.

$30 \div 6 =$

There are _____ boxes.

2. Complete the division sentences.

(a)

6 ÷ 2 =   6 ÷ 3 =

(b)
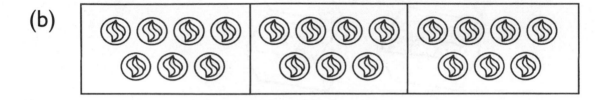

21 ÷ 3 =   21 ÷ 7 =

(c)
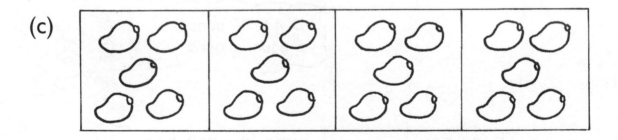

20 ÷ 4 =   20 ÷ 5 =

(d)

☆☆☆☆
☆☆☆☆☆

☆☆☆☆
☆☆☆☆☆

18 ÷ 2 =   18 ÷ 9 =

3. Write two division sentences.

(a)
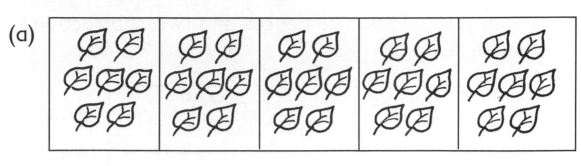

$$\boxed{} \div \boxed{} = \boxed{} \qquad \boxed{} \div \boxed{} = \boxed{}$$

(b)

$$\boxed{} \div \boxed{} = \boxed{} \qquad \boxed{} \div \boxed{} = \boxed{}$$

4. Write two multiplication sentences and two division sentences.

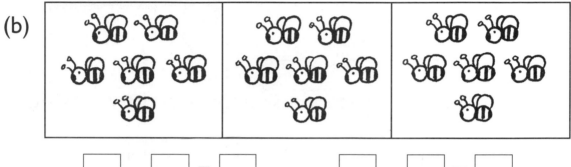

$$\boxed{} \times \boxed{} = \boxed{} \qquad \boxed{} \times \boxed{} = \boxed{}$$

$$\boxed{} \div \boxed{} = \boxed{} \qquad \boxed{} \div \boxed{} = \boxed{}$$

REVIEW 5

1. Write two addition sentences and two subtraction sentences.

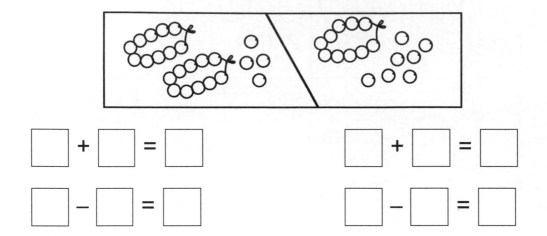

☐ + ☐ = ☐   ☐ + ☐ = ☐

☐ − ☐ = ☐   ☐ − ☐ = ☐

2. Write two multiplication sentences and two division sentences.

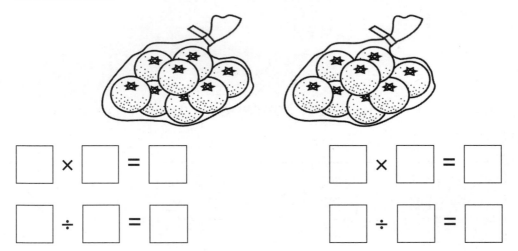

☐ × ☐ = ☐   ☐ × ☐ = ☐

☐ ÷ ☐ = ☐   ☐ ÷ ☐ = ☐

3. Write the missing numbers.

(a)

750	740		720		700	

(b)

392		592		792		992

4. Add or subtract.

(a) $400 + 60 + 5 =$
(b) $253 + 8 =$
(c) $367 + 30 =$
(d) $542 + 200 =$
(e) $444 - 400 =$
(f) $672 - 7 =$
(g) $798 - 60 =$
(h) $999 - 800 =$

5. Fill in the blanks with the given numbers.

957   980   978   969

(a) 969 is greater than _____ .

(b) 978 is less than _____ .

(c) The greatest number is _____ .

(d) The smallest number is _____ .

6. Lily bought 20 pears.
   She put 5 pears in a plastic bag.
   How many plastic bags did she use?

   ☐ ◯ ☐ = ☐

   She used _____ plastic bags.

---

7. Taylor tied 18 carrots into bundles of 6.
   How many bundles were there?

   ☐ ◯ ☐ = ☐

   There were _____ bundles.

---

8. There are 4 fish in each bowl.
   There are 5 bowls of fish.
   How many fish are there altogether?

   ☐ ◯ ☐ = ☐

   There are _____ fish altogether.

9. Huili bought 124 balloons.
   48 of them were red balloons.
   The rest were blue balloons.
   How many blue balloons were there?

   □○□ = □

   There were _____ blue balloons.

10. Meihua is 98 cm tall.
    She is 14 cm shorter than Sufen.
    What is Sufen's height?

    Sufen's height is _____ cm.

11. The total weight of two apples is 290 g.
    One apple weighs 132 g.
    How much does the other apple weigh?

    The other apple weighs _____ g.

EXERCISE 40

1. Count by twos.

 $2 \times 1 =$

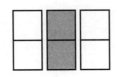 $2 \times 2 =$

 $2 \times 3 =$

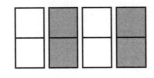 $2 \times 4 =$

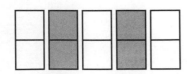 $2 \times 5 =$

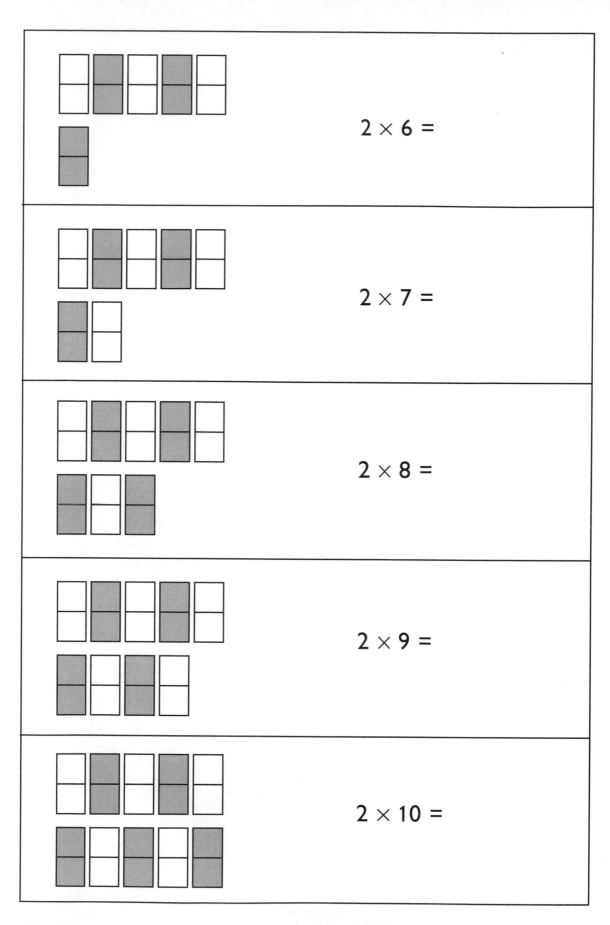

$2 \times 6 =$

$2 \times 7 =$

$2 \times 8 =$

$2 \times 9 =$

$2 \times 10 =$

2. Count the stones by twos.

Start

2

4

6

116

3. Fill in the blanks.

1 motorcycle has 2 wheels.

2 motorcycles have _____ wheels.

3 motorcycles have _____ wheels.

4 motorcycles have _____ wheels.

5 motorcycles have _____ wheels.

6 motorcycles have _____ wheels.

7 motorcycles have _____ wheels.

8 motorcycles have _____ wheels.

9 motorcycles have _____ wheels.

10 motorcycles have _____ wheels.

EXERCISE 41

1. There are 2 apples on each plate.

   $2 \times 3 =$

   There are _____ apples altogether.

2. There are 2 fish in each bowl.

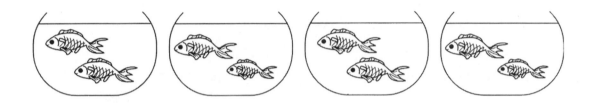

   $2 \times 4 =$

   There are _____ fish altogether.

3. There are 2 candles on each cake.

   $2 \times 5 =$

   There are _____ candles altogether.

4. There are 2 keys on a key chain.
   How many keys are there on 6 key chains?

   $2 \times 6 =$

   There are _____ keys altogether.

---

5. There are 2 straws in a glass.
   How many straws are there in 7 glasses?

   $\boxed{} \times \boxed{} = \boxed{}$

   There are _____ straws altogether.

---

6. There are 2 papayas in a basket.
   How many papayas are there in 8 baskets?

   $\boxed{} \times \boxed{} = \boxed{}$

   There are _____ papayas altogether.

EXERCISE 42

1. Complete the multiplication sentences.

(a)

2 more

$2 \times 3 = 6$

$2 \times 4 =$

(b)

$2 \times 5 = 10$

$2 \times 6 =$

(c)

$2 \times 7 =$

$2 \times 8 =$

2. Complete the multiplication sentences.

$2 \times 1 = 2$

+2

$2 \times 2 = 4$

+2

$2 \times 3 =$

+2

$2 \times 4 =$

+2

$2 \times 5 =$

+2

$2 \times 6 =$

+2

$2 \times 7 =$

+2

$2 \times 8 =$

+2

$2 \times 9 =$

+2

$2 \times 10 =$

EXERCISE 43

1. Match.

Bat	Ball
2×2	2
2×3	4
2×1	6
2×6	8
2×4	10
2×9	12
2×5	14
2×7	16
2×10	18
2×8	20

EXERCISE 44

1. Complete the multiplication sentences.

(a)

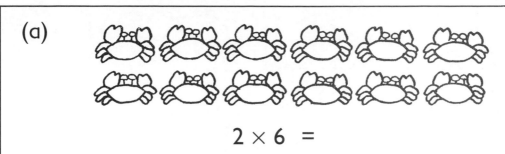

$2 \times 6 =$

$6 \times 2 =$

(b)

$2 \times 7 =$

$7 \times 2 =$

(c)

$2 \times 9 =$

$9 \times 2 =$

(d)

$2 \times 10 =$

$10 \times 2 =$

2. Match.

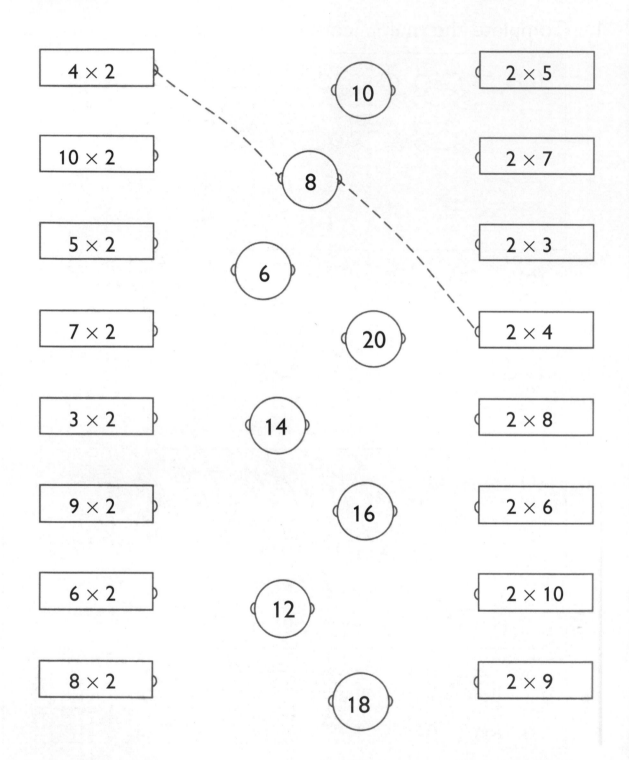

EXERCISE 45

1. Multiply.

2. Multiply.

3 × 2   6

2 × 8

6 × 2

4 × 2

9 × 2

2 × 7

2 × 10

5 × 2

2 × 4

8 × 2

2 × 9

2 × 6

EXERCISE 46

1. Melissa bought 2 boxes of buns.
   There were 8 buns in each box.
   How many buns did she buy?

   $$2 \times 8 =$$

   She bought _____ buns.

2. Peter bought 6 toy cars.
   Each toy car cost $2.
   How much did he pay?

   $\square \times \square = \square$

   He paid $ _____ .

3. Mrs. Banks has 3 children.
   She buys 2 T-shirts for each of them.
   How many T-shirts does she buy?

   $\square \times \square = \square$

   She buys _____ T-shirts.

4. Peter bought 2 tins of cookies.
   Each tin cost $7.
   How much did he pay?

   He paid $ _____ .

5. Mrs. Fu bought 5 tins of milk powder.
   There were 2 kg of milk powder in each tin.
   How many kilograms of milk powder did she buy?

   She bought _____ kg of milk powder.

6. The length of one side of the square is 2 m.
   What is the total length of the 4 sides of the square?

   2 m

   The total length is _____ m.

EXERCISE 47

1. Count by threes.

 $3 \times 1 =$

 $3 \times 2 =$

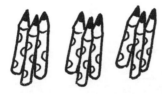 $3 \times 3 =$

 $3 \times 4 =$

 $3 \times 5 =$

$3 \times 6 =$

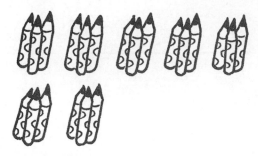

$3 \times 7 =$

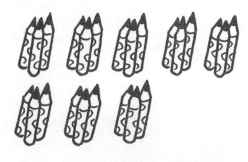

$3 \times 8 =$

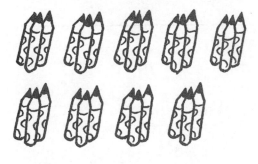

$3 \times 9 =$

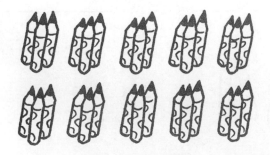

$3 \times 10 =$

2. Count the flowers by threes.

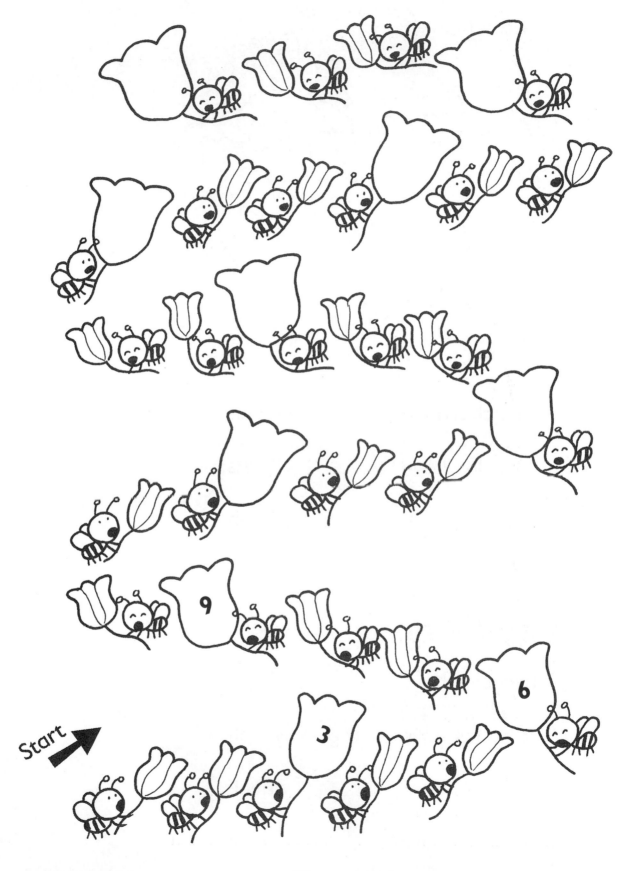

EXERCISE 48

1. Fill in the blanks.

1 tricycle has 3 wheels.

2 tricycles have _____ wheels.

3 tricycles have _____ wheels.

4 tricycles have _____ wheels.

5 tricycles have _____ wheels.

6 tricycles have _____ wheels.

7 tricycles have _____ wheels.

8 tricycles have _____ wheels.

9 tricycles have _____ wheels.

10 tricycles have _____ wheels.

2. Complete the tables.

(a) A bicycle has 2 wheels.

Number of bicycles	1	2	4	6	8
Number of wheels	2				

(b) A triangle has 3 sides.

Number of triangles	1	2	5	7	9
Number of sides	3				

(c) Pies for sale   Cakes for sale
   $2 each $3 each

Number of pies	Cost
1	$2
2	$4
3	
5	
7	
9	
10	

Number of cakes	Cost
1	$3
2	$6
3	
4	
6	
8	
10	

EXERCISE 49

1. Draw 3 lines across and 2 lines down.
    Count the number of crossings.

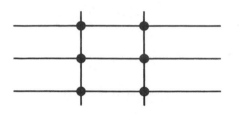

3 × 2 =

2 × 3 =

2. Complete the multiplication sentences.

    (a)
    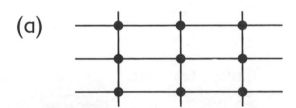

    3 × 3 =

    (b)

    3 × 4 =

    4 × 3 =

    (c)
    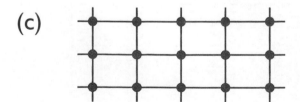

    3 × 5 =

    5 × 3 =

3. Complete the multiplication sentences.

(a)

☆☆☆☆☆☆
☆☆☆☆☆☆
☆☆☆☆☆☆

3 × 6 =

6 × 3 =

(b)

3 × 7 =

7 × 3 =

(c)

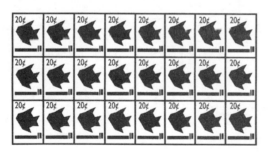

3 × 8 =

8 × 3 =

(d)

😊😊😊😊😊😊😊😊😊
😊😊😊😊😊😊😊😊😊
😊😊😊😊😊😊😊😊😊

3 × 9 =

9 × 3 =

EXERCISE 50

1. Match.

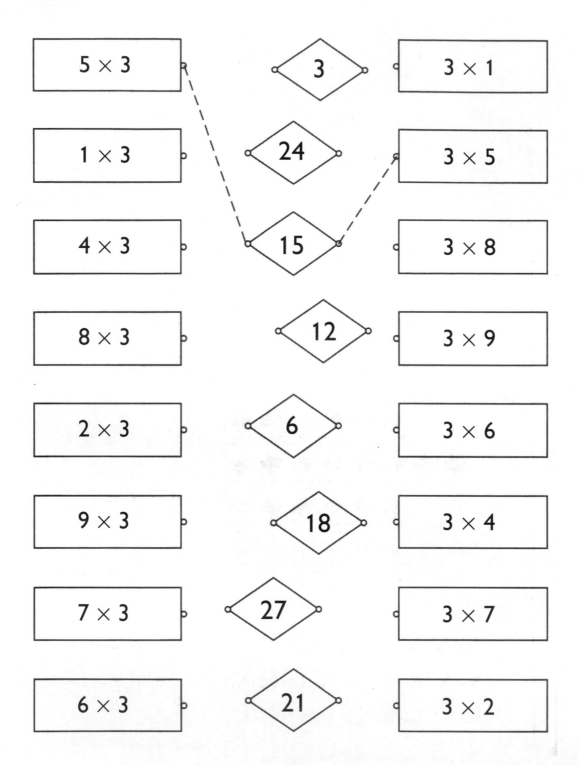

2. Match.

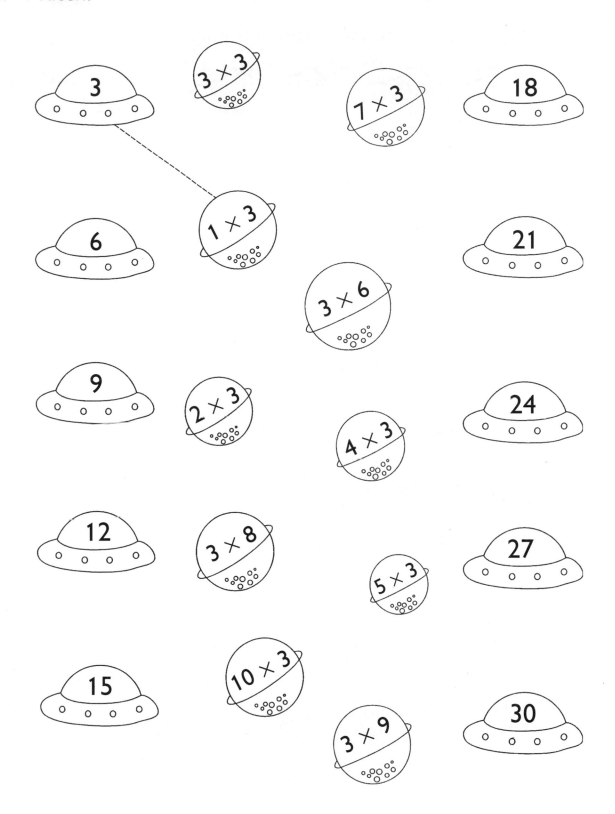

EXERCISE 51

1. Complete the multiplication sentences.

(a)

$3 \times 3 = 9$

$3 \times 4 =$

3 more

(b)

$3 \times 5 = 15$

$3 \times 6 =$

(c)

$3 \times 8 =$

$3 \times 9 =$

2. Complete the multiplication sentences.

$3 \times 1 = 3$

+3

$3 \times 2 = 6$

+3

$3 \times 3 =$

+3

$3 \times 4 =$

+3

$3 \times 5 =$

+3

$3 \times 6 =$

+3

$3 \times 7 =$

+3

$3 \times 8 =$

+3

$3 \times 9 =$

+3

$3 \times 10 =$

EXERCISE 52

1. Complete the multiplication sentences.

(a)

$3 \times 5 = 15$

$3 \times 4 =$

3 less

(b)

$3 \times 7 = 21$

$3 \times 6 =$

(c)

$3 \times 10 =$

$3 \times 9 =$

2. Complete the multiplication sentences.

$3 \times 10 = 30$

-3

$3 \times 9 = 27$

-3

$3 \times 8 =$

-3

$3 \times 7 =$

-3

$3 \times 6 =$

-3

$3 \times 5 =$

-3

$3 \times 4 =$

-3

$3 \times 3 =$

-3

$3 \times 2 =$

-3

$3 \times 1 =$

EXERCISE 53

1. Multiply.

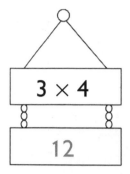

3 × 4

12

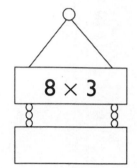

8 × 3

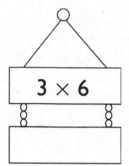

3 × 6

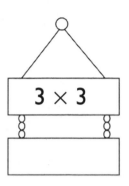

3 × 3

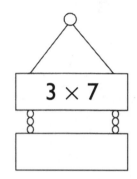

3 × 7

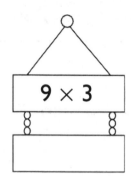

9 × 3

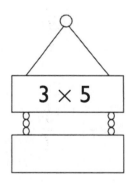

3 × 5

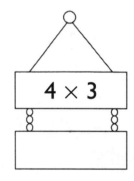

4 × 3

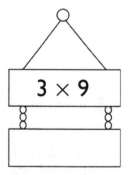

3 × 9

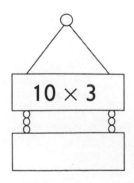

10 × 3

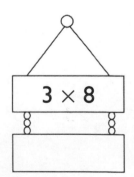

3 × 8

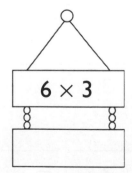

6 × 3

EXERCISE 54

1. Mrs. Anderson bought 3 trays of eggs.
    There were 10 eggs on each tray.
    How many eggs did she buy?

    She bought _____ eggs.

2. Maria bought 3 pieces of ribbon.
    Each piece of ribbon was 8 m long.
    How many meters of ribbon did she buy?

    She bought _____ m of ribbon.

3. Warner bought 3 storybooks.
    Each storybook cost $5.
    How much did he pay?

    He paid $ _____ .

4. There are 7 days in a week.
   How many days are there in 3 weeks?

   There are _____ days in 3 weeks.

5. The length of each side of the triangle is 9 in.
   What is the total length of the 3 sides of the triangle?

   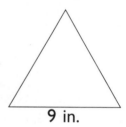

   9 in.

   The total length is _____ in.

6. A bag of sugar weighs 3 kg.
   What is the total weight of 6 such bags of sugar?

   The total weight is _____ kg.

EXERCISE 55

1. Multiply.

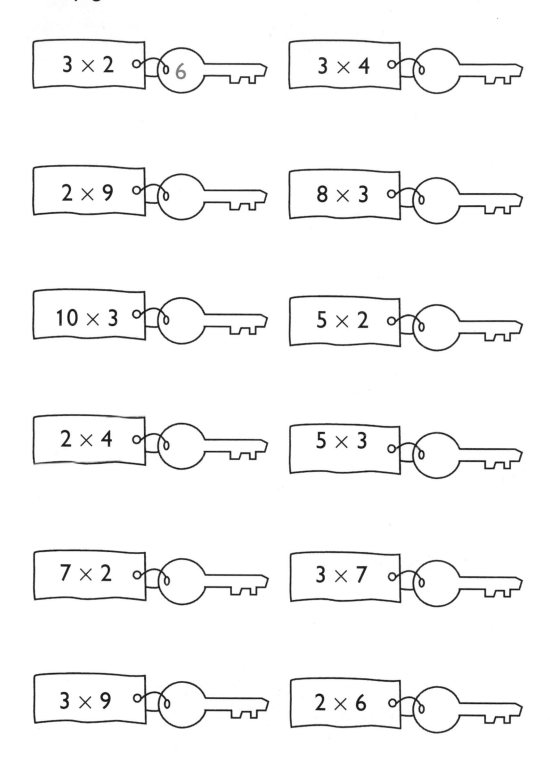

2. There are **3** rooms in one house.
    How many rooms are there in **8** houses?

    There are _____ rooms in **8** houses.

---

3. Nathan eats **3** oranges a day.
    How many oranges does he eat in a week?

    7 days in a week

    He eats _____ oranges in a week.

---

4. Mr. Rowley buys **2** copies of newspapers a day.
    How many copies of newspapers does he buy in a week?

    He buys _____ copies of newspapers in a week.

5. Leigh bought 2 bags of rice.
   Each bag of rice weighed 10 kg.
   How many kilograms of rice did she buy?

   She bought _____ kg of rice.

6. Lily tied 8 packages.
   She used 2 m of string for each package.
   How many meters of string did she use altogether?

   She used _____ m of spring altogether.

7. Sara bought 3 kg of pineapples.
   1 kg of pineapples cost $6.
   How much did she pay?

   She paid $ _____ .

EXERCISE 56

1. Write the missing numbers.

$1 \times 2 = 2$

$2 \div 2 = \underline{\hspace{1cm}}$

$2 \times 2 = 4$

$4 \div 2 = \underline{\hspace{1cm}}$

$5 \times 2 = 10$

$10 \div 2 = \underline{\hspace{1cm}}$

$\underline{\hspace{1cm}} \times 2 = 16$

$16 \div 2 = \underline{\hspace{1cm}}$

$\underline{\hspace{1cm}} \times 2 = 6$

$6 \div 2 = \underline{\hspace{1cm}}$

$\underline{\hspace{1cm}} \times 2 = 18$

$18 \div 2 = \underline{\hspace{1cm}}$

$\underline{\hspace{1cm}} \times 2 = 20$

$20 \div 2 = \underline{\hspace{1cm}}$

$\underline{\hspace{1cm}} \times 2 = 8$

$8 \div 2 = \underline{\hspace{1cm}}$

$\underline{\hspace{1cm}} \times 2 = 12$

$12 \div 2 = \underline{\hspace{1cm}}$

$\underline{\hspace{1cm}} \times 2 = 14$

$14 \div 2 = \underline{\hspace{1cm}}$

2. Match.

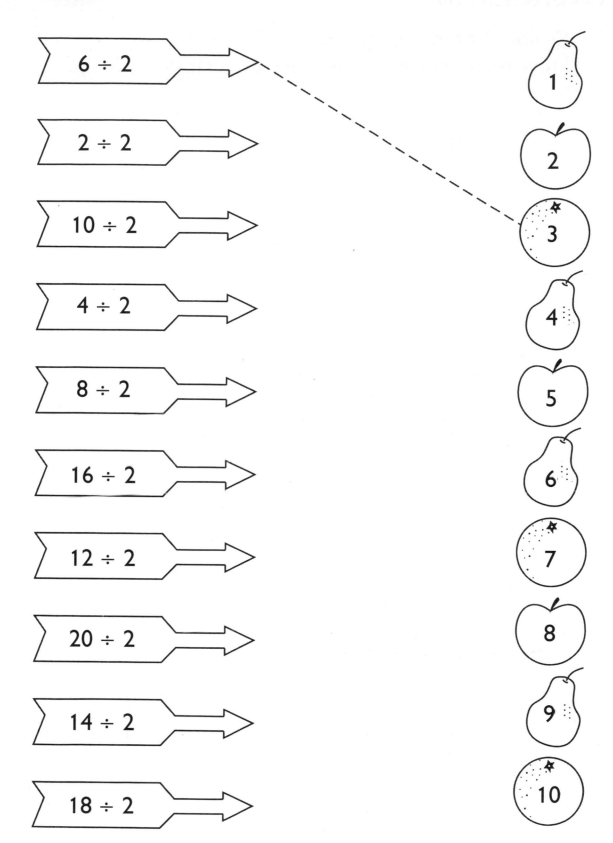

$6 \div 2$

$2 \div 2$

$10 \div 2$

$4 \div 2$

$8 \div 2$

$16 \div 2$

$12 \div 2$

$20 \div 2$

$14 \div 2$

$18 \div 2$

1
2
3
4
5
6
7
8
9
10

EXERCISE 57

1. Divide 8 children equally into 2 groups.
   How many children are there in each group?

   There are _____ children in each group.

2. Sumin puts 10 buns equally into 2 boxes.
   How many buns are there in each box?

   There are _____ buns in each box.

3. David and Tom share a box of 12 pencils equally.
   How many pencils does each boy get?

   Each boy gets _____ pencils.

4. Rebecca arranged 20 chairs in 2 rows.
   She put the same number of chairs in each row.
   How many chairs were there in each row?

   There were _____ chairs in each row.

5. Mr. Campbell has a rope 14 m long.
   He cuts it into equal pieces.
   Each piece is 2 m long.
   How many pieces of rope does he get?

   He gets _____ pieces of rope.

6. Cameron bought 16 pies.
   He put 2 pies in a box.
   How many boxes did he use?

   He used _____ boxes.

EXERCISE 58

1. Write the missing numbers.

$1 \times 3 = 3$	$3 \div 3 = \underline{\quad}$
$2 \times 3 = 6$	$6 \div 3 = \underline{\quad}$
$\underline{\quad} \times 3 = 12$	$12 \div 3 = \underline{\quad}$
$\underline{\quad} \times 3 = 15$	$15 \div 3 = \underline{\quad}$
$\underline{\quad} \times 3 = 9$	$9 \div 3 = \underline{\quad}$
$\underline{\quad} \times 3 = 30$	$30 \div 3 = \underline{\quad}$
$\underline{\quad} \times 3 = 21$	$21 \div 3 = \underline{\quad}$
$\underline{\quad} \times 3 = 27$	$27 \div 3 = \underline{\quad}$
$\underline{\quad} \times 3 = 18$	$18 \div 3 = \underline{\quad}$
$\underline{\quad} \times 3 = 24$	$24 \div 3 = \underline{\quad}$

2. Match.

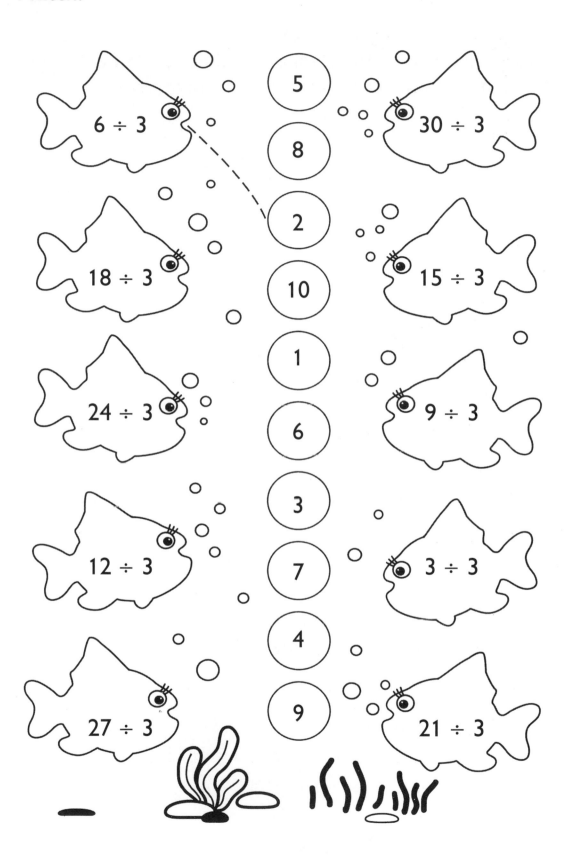

EXERCISE 59

1. 24 children line up in 3 rows.
   There are the same number of children in each row.
   How many children are there in each row?

   There are _____ children in each row.

2. Juan saved $18 in 3 weeks.
   He saved the same amount each week.
   How much did he save each week?

   He saved $ _____ each week.

3. Carlos cut a wire 12 yd long into 3 equal pieces.
   Find the length of each piece of wire.

   The length of each piece of wire was _____ yd.

4. Emily needs 3 m of cloth to make a dress.
   How many dresses can she make with 15 m of cloth?

   She can make _____ dresses.

5. Mr. Ray placed 27 pears equally on 3 plates.
   How many pears were there on each plate?

   There were _____ pears on each plate.

6. Ryan paid $21 for 3 kg of papayas.
   Find the cost of 1 kg of papayas.

   The cost of 1 kg of papayas was $ _____ .

EXERCISE 60

1. Match.

Rabbits (left column): 3, 2, 1, 4, 7

Carrots (middle column): 15 ÷ 3, 12 ÷ 2, 9 ÷ 3, 2 ÷ 2, 6 ÷ 3, 14 ÷ 2, 20 ÷ 2, 27 ÷ 3, 12 ÷ 3, 16 ÷ 2

Rabbits (right column): 6, 5, 10, 8, 9

2.

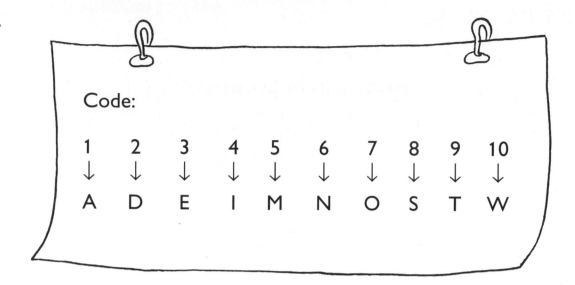

Code:

1	2	3	4	5	6	7	8	9	10
↓	↓	↓	↓	↓	↓	↓	↓	↓	↓
A	D	E	I	M	N	O	S	T	W

Divide.

Then use the code above to change the answers into letters.

You will find a message.

6 ÷ 3	14 ÷ 2
2	
D	

12 ÷ 2	21 ÷ 3	27 ÷ 3

20 ÷ 2	3 ÷ 3	24 ÷ 3	18 ÷ 2	9 ÷ 3

27 ÷ 3	12 ÷ 3	15 ÷ 3	6 ÷ 2

EXERCISE 61

1. 3 lb of prawns cost $24.
   What is the cost of 1 lb of prawns?

   The cost of 1 lb of prawns is $ _____ .

2. Nicole puts 18 cakes equally into 2 boxes.
   How many cakes are there in each box?

   There are _____ cakes in each box.

3. Emma bought 18 notebooks at 3 for $1.
   How much did she pay?

   She paid $ _____ .

4. 1 kg of tomatoes costs $2.
    How many kilograms of tomatoes cost $12?

    _____ kg of tomatoes cost $12.

5. David spent $27 in 3 weeks.
    He spent the same amount of money each week.
    How much money did he spend each week?

    He spent $ _____ each week.

6. Sufen and Lily shared the cost of a present equally.
    The present cost $16.
    How much did each girl pay?

    Each girl paid $ _____ .

EXERCISE 62

1. Multiply or divide.

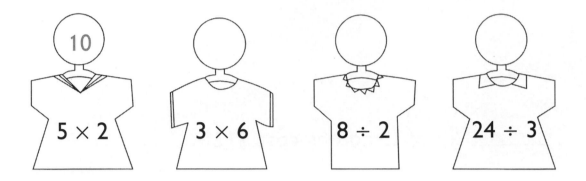

5 × 2   3 × 6   8 ÷ 2   24 ÷ 3

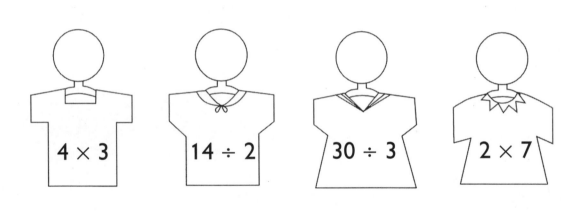

4 × 3   14 ÷ 2   30 ÷ 3   2 × 7

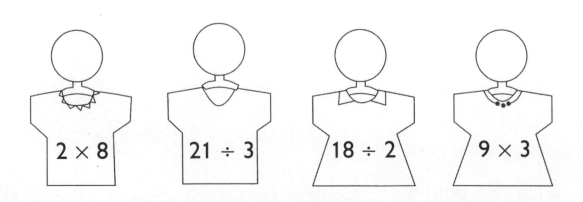

2 × 8   21 ÷ 3   18 ÷ 2   9 × 3

2. The total length of 3 equal pieces of string is 15 cm. What is the length of each piece of string?

The length of each piece of string is _____ cm.

3. There are 3 bars of soap in a bundle. How many bars of soap are there altogether in 7 bundles?

There are _____ bars of soap altogether.

4. Ali, Sumin and Samy each bought 4 toy cars. How many toy cars did they buy altogether?

They bought _____ toy cars altogether.

5. A tailor wants to make 6 dresses.
   She needs 3 yd of cloth to make a dress.
   How many yards of cloth does she need altogether?

   She needs _____ yd of cloth.

6. 3 concert tickets cost $24.
   Each ticket costs the same amount of money.
   What is the cost of each ticket?

   The cost of each ticket is $ _____ .

7. David and John spent the same amount of money at a carnival.
   They spent $18 altogether.
   How much money did each boy spend?

   Each boy spent $ _____ .

REVIEW 6

1. Write the numbers in words.

    (a) 857 _____

    (b) 644 _____

2. Write two multiplication sentences and two division sentences.

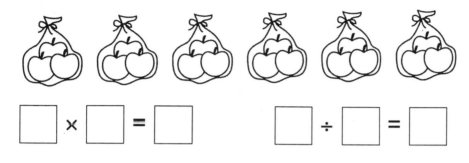

    □ × □ = □   □ ÷ □ = □

    □ × □ = □   □ ÷ □ = □

3. Use the given numbers and signs to write a number sentence.

    (a) _____

50	406	456
	−	=

    (b) _____

275	600	325
	+	=

    (c) _____

3	27	9
	×	=

    (d) _____

2	18	9
	÷	=

4. Complete the number patterns.

950	960	970		990	
	959			989	
	958				
				987	
		966	976		

5. Fill in the blanks.

(a) 13 − 6 = _____

   6 less than 13 is _____ .

(b) 15 − 9 = _____

   _____ is 9 less than 15.

6. Arrange the numbers in order.
   Begin with the smallest.

   _____

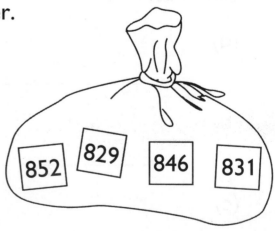

   852   829   846   831

7. Write the missing numbers.
   (a) 300 + ☐ = 307
   (b) 652 − ☐ = 602

8. Add or subtract.

544 − 104	692 − 596	408 − 178
320 − 217	629 − 179	800 − 164
140 + 190	265 + 87	694 + 146
200 40 + 80	300 60 + 95	420 30 + 68

Color the spaces that contain the answers.

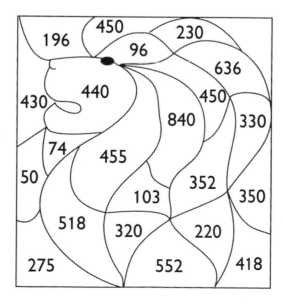

9. Follow the arrows.
   Fill in the missing numbers.

START   **CHECKPOINT**

(8)

↓ + 2   ↑ + 2   ÷ 2 →   (10)

( )   ( )   ↓ − 2

↓ + 2   ↑ × 2   ( )

( )   ( )   ↓ − 2

↓ ÷ 2   ↑ + 2   ( )

( )   ( )   ↓ × 2

↓ − 2   ↑ ÷ 2   ( )

( )   ( )   ↓ − 2

↓ × 2   ↑ − 2   ( )

( )   × 2 →   (16)   ↓ × 2

                                            (20)

CHECKPOINT   **END**

10. Matthew sold 402 mangoes on Sunday.
He sold 35 fewer mangoes on Monday than on Sunday.
How many mangoes did he sell on Monday?

He sold _____ mangoes on Monday.

---

11. A shopkeeper sold 6 toy airplanes at $4 each.
How much money did he collect?

He collected $ _____ .

---

12. 24 soldiers lined up in 3 rows.
There were an equal number of soldiers in each row.
How many soldiers were there in each row?

There were _____ soldiers in each row.

13. There are 460 chickens and 295 ducks in a farm.
    How many more chickens than ducks are there?

    There are _____ more chickens than ducks.

_____

14. Mrs. Jackson puts 18 pastries equally into 2 boxes.
    How many pastries are there in each box?

    There are _____ pastries in each box.

_____

15. After selling 285 sticks of satay, Mrs. Wu had 168 sticks
    of satay left.
    How many sticks of satay did she have at first?

    She had _____ sticks of satay at first.

REVIEW 7

1. Write the numbers.

    (a) Five hundred fifty _____

    (b) Nine hundred twenty-nine _____

2. Write the numbers in words.

    (a) 744 _____

    (b) 806 _____

3. Write **greater than (>)** or **less than (<)** in the blank.

    (a) 199 is _____ 201.

    (b) 379 is _____ 382.

    (c) 480 is _____ 469.

    (d) 566 is _____ 506.

    (e) 734 is _____ 704.

    (f) 908 is _____ 980.

4. Fill in the blanks.

    (a) 800 + 70 + 9 = _____

    (b) 700 + 60 = _____

    (c) 500 + 4 = _____

    (d) 400 + _____ = 490

    (e) 677 − 70 = _____

    (f) 486 − _____ = 476

5. Fill in the blanks.

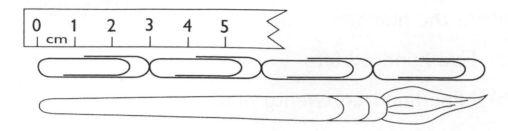

(a) The length of each paper clip is _____ cm.

(b) The length of the brush is _____ cm.

6. Fill in the blanks.

(a) The pumpkin weighs _____ kg.

(b) 1 kg of pumpkin costs $3.

The pumpkin costs $ _____ .

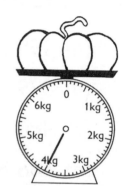

7. Fill in the blanks with the correct units.

lb, oz, yd, ft, in.

(a) Mr. Owens weighs about 150 _____ .

(b) Justin's height is about 38 _____ .

(c) After dinner, Lily and her brother ate about
9 _____ of grapes.

(d) The height of a door is about 2 _____ .

(e) The length of this book is about 1 _____ .

8. Add or subtract.

(a) $\begin{array}{r} 324 \\ + 149 \\ \hline \end{array}$	(b) $\begin{array}{r} 440 \\ + 76 \\ \hline \end{array}$
(c) $\begin{array}{r} 569 \\ + 283 \\ \hline \end{array}$	(d) $\begin{array}{r} 378 \\ + 422 \\ \hline \end{array}$
(e) $\begin{array}{r} 594 \\ - 254 \\ \hline \end{array}$	(f) $\begin{array}{r} 300 \\ - 174 \\ \hline \end{array}$
(g) $\begin{array}{r} 406 \\ - 48 \\ \hline \end{array}$	(h) $\begin{array}{r} 704 \\ - 129 \\ \hline \end{array}$

9. Multiply or divide.

(a) $3 \times 2 =$	(b) $5 \times 3 =$
(c) $7 \times 3 =$	(d) $9 \times 2 =$
(e) $3 \times 3 =$	(f) $2 \times 5 =$
(g) $2 \times 8 =$	(h) $3 \times 9 =$
(i) $2 \div 2 =$	(j) $6 \div 3 =$
(k) $10 \div 2 =$	(l) $18 \div 2 =$
(m) $3 \div 3 =$	(n) $15 \div 3 =$
(o) $16 \div 2 =$	(p) $21 \div 3 =$

10. The total weight of 2 bags of sugar is 12 lb.
    Each bag has the same weight.
    What is the weight of each bag?

    The weight of each bag is ＿＿＿＿＿＿ lb.

11. 1 kg of mangoes costs $3.
    Lindsey buys 6 kg of mangoes.
    How much does she pay?

    She pays $ ＿＿＿＿＿＿ .

12. The total length of 2 pieces of rope is 18 yd.
    One piece of rope is 3 yd long.
    What is the length of the other piece of rope?

    The length of the other piece of rope is ＿＿＿＿＿＿ yd.

13. Raju had $500.
    After buying a camera, he had $264 left.
    What was the cost of the camera?

    The cost of the camera was $ _____ .

14. Sumin has 85 marbles.
    He needs another 46 marbles to fill a bottle.
    How many marbles can the bottle hold?

    The bottle can hold _____ marbles.

15. There are 420 workers in a factory.
    285 of them are men.
    How many women are there?

    There are _____ women.

BLANK

BLANK